History of China

Deng Yinke

translation by Martha Avery and Pan Yue

CHINA
INTERCONTINENTAL
PRESS

JOURNEY INTO CHINA

Counsellor: Cai Wu
General Director: Li Bing
Chief Editors: Guo Changjian & Li Xiangping
Deputy Chief Editor: Wu Wei

◇◇◇

图书在版编目（CIP）数据

历史之旅：英文/邓荫柯著；潘岳译.—北京：五洲传播出版社，2007.8（2011.11重印）
（中国之旅）
ISBN 978-7-5085-1098-9

I. 历…
II. ①邓… ②潘…
III. 中国-历史-英文
IV. K2

中国版本图书馆CIP数据核字（2007）第064533号

HISTORY OF CHINA

Author: Deng Yinke
Translator: Martha Avery & Pan Yue
Planner: Feng Lingyu
Project Director: Deng Jinhui
Executive Editor: Gao Lei
Art Director: Tian Lin
Photo Credit: Imagine China, China Foto Press, China Intercontinental Press
Publisher: China Intercontinental Press (Tower B-7, Shengchanli Building, No.31, Beisanhuan Zhonglu, Haidian District, Beijing 100088, China)
Printer: Beijing Picture in Picture Printing Co., Ltd.
Tel: 86-10-82004593
Website: www.cicc.org.cn
Edition: Aug. 2007, 1st edition, Nov. 2011, 4th print run
Format: 787×1092mm 1/16
Signatures: 10.875
Words: 42,000
Print Run: 16,001-18,500
Price: RMB 96.00 (yuan)

Contents

Prologue

China has a long and brilliant history. Its documented history is coherent for 3,000 years and its undocumented history is clearly inherited orally for 5,000 years. Archyological discoveries can date back its history to 7,000 years and trace all stages of human development to 500,000 years. Its history has never been interrupted or deminished, and it's certainly not a civilization suddenly discovered after many decades or dynasties. Although China has gone through stagnation and aggression in the modern times, she nevertheless has been playing an important role at the heart of the world's stage. Her history and culture, together with her rivers and mountains, possess infinite charm, which is also the soft power of China. The world has been observing the revival miracle of China for the past thirty years, at the same time paying more and more attention to China's unique history and culture. People try to find the historic origin of China's progress, and they try to find solutions and lessons for the Occident's decline. The glory resides both in her history and in her present. The world's spotlight has focused on this ancient and young country. Thousands of foreign friends come to visit China to see her present and her past. They are attracted by her social development as well as by her beautiful landscapes.

In this book I will take the readers to a journey into the Chinese history, to visit the historic sites and ruins, to meet the historic figures, to feel the glory of history itself. The relics include palaces, temples, mausoleums, ancient housings, steles, sculptures, frescos, fortifications, irrigation works, ancient roadways and ferries, archaeological sites, and cultural relics. They are scattered all over China's vast territory and indicate different historical periods. They just about cover all the stages and dynasties of the Chinese history. They are located specifically near and around cities like Beijing, Xi'an, Luoyang, Kaifeng, Nanjing, Hangzhou, Anyang, Chengdu, and Qufu. I have also included some very important works which weigh as much as the historic sites and can be regarded as the starting point of a certain piece of history. At each historic site, there are often cultural relics from different times. For example in Beijing, there is the Zhoukoudian site from ancient times and there are also palaces of the Ming Dynasty and the Qing Dynasty. There is the Great Wall that was built in the Qin Dynasty and lasted through the Ming Dynasty till today. Around Xi'an, there is the Banpo site from pre-history as well as mausoleums from the Qin Dynasty and Han Dynasty, and palaces of the Han Dynasty and Tang Dynasty. These historic sites have become indispensable parts of the Chinese landscape and famous touring sites. This book introduces the places and what happened at these places in history at the same time. So it's a historic touring guide and a geographic history pamphlet. The characteristic differentiate it from general touring routes and is a good reference for a journey into the Chinese history.

I have selected twenty some significant historic sites to introduce thoroughly. Connecting these sites one can find the outline of the Chinese history. When we travel to a certain famous historic city, we can also recognize its positioning and the role it played in history. Thus, we get an experience of cruising on the river of history.

Zhoukoudian: the Dawn of Early Man

Discovered in the early 20th century, the Zhoukoudian site near Beijing provided an extremely rich fund of fossilized materials of early hominids. These were found in conjunction with extensive botanical fossils. From intensive study of these materials, we have gained an understanding of mankind's early period, and we are able in a sense to listen to the distant echoing voices of our forebears. The site is one of the most outstanding among a

Statue of the Peking Ape-man.

number of sites relating to ancient hominids in China, others including the Yuanmou Man site in Yunnan and the Lantian Man site in Shaanxi. The discoveries at Zhoukoudian helped in providing humanity with a much clearer understanding of man's development. Most early hominid sites in the world are located in remote and wild mountainous areas. Zhoukoudian is near an international capital, the city of Beijing. It provides a rare opportunity to those friends who come from all over the world to understand the culture of ancient man, and at the same time to begin to understand the long course of China's civilization.

The "Peking Man Site," as it is called, is located fifty kilometers to the southwest of the city of Beijing, in the Long-gu or "Dragon-Bone" Mountains of the Fangshan District. In the early twentieth century, foreign scholars who were doing research in China began to take an interest in the areas where local farmers gathered "dragon bones" which they used as a kind of medicinal cure. The Austrian paleontologist O. Zdansky and the Canadian surgeon, Davidson Black, as well as others, believed that

Excavations of the Zhoukoudian site.

Cave of the ape men at Zhoukoudian site.

Palaeoanthropology scholar Jia Lanpo (1908–2001).

these "dragon bones" might be the fossilized remains of some rare ancient plant. Excavations were carried out at Zhoukoudian, under the supervision of foreign scholars and Chinese botanists and geologists such as Weng Wenhao and Yang Zhongjian. Fossilized teeth that appeared similar to those of early hominids were unearthed. In 1929, as a result of painstaking effort, the young paleontologist Pei Wenzhong excavated a nearly complete cranium and lower jaw and skeleton, a discovery that amazed the whole world. Scholars called the remains "Peking Man," and went on to discover stone artifacts, bone artifacts and evidence of the use of fire, proving that hominids were active in what is now the Beijing region five hundred thousand years ago. In 1930, scholars excavated further fossilized remains of early hominids from around 200,000 years ago. Found at the upper part of Dragon-bone Mountain, these were given the name "Mountain-top Cave Man."

In November 1936, within the space of one month a worker named Jia Lanpo, untutored in archaeology at the time, further discovered three craniums of Peking Man, thereby making a tremendous contribution to research. In 1937, as the Japanese were mobilizing a comprehensive invasion of China as prelude to war, three men who had been guarding Zhoukoudian were killed by Japanese soldiers. At the same time the supremely valuable first skull of

Peking Man went missing. Later, remains of a hominid intermediate between "Peking Man" and "Mountain-top Cave Man" were discovered at Zhoukoudian, indicating the continuing presence and development of Peking Man at the site. These discoveries and this research cemented the unique position of the site in global paleo-archaeological studies. Six early hominid cranium fossils were eventually excavated at Zhoukoudian, plus twelve fragments of skulls, fifteen lower jawbones, 157 pieces of teeth, and fragments of skeletons belonging to more than forty persons, both female and male, old and young. In addition, some 100,000 stone-tool artifacts were excavated, and a hearth where fire was used and stones and bones had been charred. The average cranial capacity of Peking Man was 1,088 millilitres (that of modern man is 1,400 millilitres). It is estimated that Peking Man stood 156 centimeters high on average (male) and 150 cm (female). Peking Man belonged to the stone age, and the primary methods of working stone tools

Several archeologists who contributed greatly to the discovery of the Peking Ape-man were buried at Longgu Mountain. They are Yang Zhongjian, Pei Wenzhong, Jia Lanpo, etc.

Burnt bone.

Zhoukoudian Site Museum.

The skull fossil of the Peking Man, exhibited at the Zhoukoudian Site Museum from September 21, 2003; The piece of skull is a frontal bone, discovered in May 1966.

were chipping, flaking, and very occasionally drilling. To this date, Peking Man is the earliest hominid discovered to have used fire; he also hunted large animals. The life expectancy of Peking Man was relatively short—it is estimated that 68.2% of individuals died before the age of 14, and less than 4.5% of individuals lived to be over 50.

A museum was erected at the Zhoukoudian Peking Man site in 1953, to exhibit cultural artifacts from the excavations in the area. The museum covered 4,000 square meters, and also extended protection to an area of two square kilometers. The exhibition at that time was basically devoted to four main areas: Peking Ape-Man, Peking Ape-man's living environment, Locations at the Excavation site, and From Ape to Man. The items exhibited in the displays were not originals; they were all reproductions made to a high degree of similarity so that they seemed authentic. The fossilized remains of animals and the hearth were authentic.

In December 1987, UNESCO listed Zhoukoudian as a World Heritage Site.

The Mausoleum of the Yellow Emperor

Leaving the capital city of Beijing, we now travel out on the high loess plateau to pay our respects to an imperial tomb in Shaanxi Province. This imperial tomb was called "Qiao Ling" or Bridge Tomb in ancient times, and is situated in the Bridge Mountains of Huangling County, Shaanxi Province. The progenitor of the Chinese people, the Yellow Emperor, is honored and recognized by this mausoleum. A stele with the inscription "Tomb of the Yellow Emperor" stands before the Altar for Offerings. At the entrance to the precinct

Earth grave at the Mausoleum of the Yellow Emperor; with "dragon drive at Bridge Hill" inscribed on the stele.

Memorial kiosk at the Mausoleum of the Yellow Emperor, with the stele of Guo Moruo's calligraphy inside.

of the tomb is an "immortals terrace" of Han Wudi. The Xuanyuan Temple, Xuanyuan being the name given to the Yellow Emperor, is located at the foot of the Bridge Mountains, and is the place where generations of sons and grandsons of the Yan clan made offerings to the Emperor. Inside the temple, the central axis of the architectural grouping includes buildings called the "Mountain Gate," "Honesty Pavilion," "Stelae Pavilion," "Ancestral Hall of Humanity," on the East side is a stelae pavision, on the west side are arrayed exhibition rooms. Sixteen ancient trees stand inside the courtyard that are over one thousand years in age. Among them, the cypress that is said to have been planted by the hand of the Emperor himself is reputed to be 5,000 years old. It well deserves the title of the world's reigning cypress tree. Surrounded by a peaceful environment of mountains and water, the tomb district is ancient and simple, conveying a sense of great and unusual majesty.

Where was the Yellow Emperor born? Where did he establish his rule, and administer his domain? According to the historian Sima Qian, of the second century BC, it was in the vicinity of Xuanyuan Hill. In the record of the Five Emperors in Sima Qian's *Historical Records* (the *Shi Ji*, finished in 91 BC), it is written that "the Yellow Emperor, son of Shaodian, surname Sun, name Xuanyuan. Resided on Xuanyuan Hill." This Xuanyuan Hill is in modern-day Xinzheng City, Henan Province. In ancient times, Xinzheng was the capital of a country named for its having bears, or "Youxiong." Shaodian, father of the Yellow Emperor, was head of the country Youxiong. Xinzheng is situated in the central part of Henan Province. In 1977, archaeologists discovered a culture that they named the Peiligang Culture at this site, evidence that ancestors of the Chinese nation lived here some 8,000 years ago. The dating of the archaeological material corresponds roughly to the time of the life of the Yellow Emperor. Other Chinese historical documents contain many references to Xuanyuan, noting that Xinzheng was the site of his rule. In the

Stone statue of the Yellow Emperor in Xuanyuan Hall.

book *Generations of Imperial Capitals*, it is recorded: "The Yellow Emperor was born at Xinzheng in the country known as Having Bears." The *Yi-tong Annals* recorded: "Xuanyuan Hill is located in Xinzheng County in Kaifeng Prefecture." In former days, a tall stone stele stood six feet high to the north of Xinzheng, at the pass leading out of town. On it were inscribed four large characters: "Site of Xuan Yuan." Since this stele was embraced by an ancient scholar tree that had grown around it, the common name for the place was "Scholar tree-embraced Stele." The temple built to commemorate the Yellow Emperor was built near this stele. By now, both stelae and temple have long since disappeared, but a new stele has been erected at the location of the old one with the same words, and the Xuanyuan Yellow Emperor Temple has been rebuilt. Sons and grandsons of the Yan-state clan come from around the world to seek the roots of their ancestry here, and to pay respects to the Xuanyuan Yellow Emperor.

The Yellow Emperor belonged to the clan with the surname of Ji, although some say his surname was Gongsun. He is said to have been the leader of the clan.

Xuanyuan Hall, in memorial of the Yellow Emperor.

According to notations in Chinese historical annals, after he defeated the Emperor of the state of Yan, he formed an alliance with the Yan Emperor, and repelled the invasion of nine tribes. He then took over from the Emperor of Yan as head of the alliance. The Emperor of Yan, as Yellow Emperor, is also known in Chinese legend as being the father of or even the god of agriculture. He invented agriculture, created agricultural tools, taught the people about sowing and reaping, and in general led the people out of the age of hunting into an agricultural age. The god of agriculture was also the god of medicine, who strode the hills collecting specimens, and who discovered which plants could treat which maladies. Because of this experimentation, he personally was seriously ill 72 times. Later, he transmitted his extensive pharmacological knowledge to the people by writing a book on pharmacopiaea, recording 365 kinds of medicinal plants. The Yellow Emperor united all the tribes in China, and built his capital at Xinzheng (some scholars believe it was elsewhere). He calculated the calendar, discovered the magnetic compass, made ships and arrows, revived

education, created musical instruments, understood the Heavenly stems and Earthly branches. The Yellow Emperor and the Emperor of Yan are both regarded as being the progenitors of the Chinese race. Chinese people therefore call themselves, "the sons and grandsons of Yan Huang."

The monument of Macao's return with Edmund Ho Hauwah's epigraph and the monument of Hongkong's return with Tung Chee-hwa's epigraph in the yard of Xuanyuan Temple.

Legend has it that the primary imperial concubine of the Yellow Emperor was named Luo, a woman who was also the ancestor of Chinese people who invented silk spinning and weaving.

Legends relating to the history of China's primordial beginnings start with the myth of Pangu splitting the heaven and earth, and creating man together with the being known as Nüwa. This corresponds to the creation myths of Western people, with God creating the earth and humankind. In China, after the creation came a period of the three "Huangs" and the five "Dis." The two words together, huang-di, form the modern Chinese word for Emperor. There are different versions of the legend, but the most common reckoning has it that the three "Huangs" or Emperors were Emperor of heaven, of earth, and of man. The five "Dis" were the Yellow Emperor

The statue of the Emperor of Yan at the Mausoleum of the Emperor of Yan in Zhuzhou, Hunan.

and then four others. Some say that the Yellow Emperor was third among the first three "Huangs," namely, the Emperor of man. Others hold that he was among the five "Dis." Either way, his high standing can be recognized. According to the *Historical Records* of Sima Qian, the Yellow Emperor had twenty-five sons, and fourteen of them received his surname. The monarchs of successive dynasties, from Xia (2070–1600 BC), Shang (1600–1046 BC), and Zhou (1046–256 BC), all regarded themselves as descendants of the Yellow Emperor. According to the *Historical Records* and also to other historical records, documentable history in China can be traced back to 2070 BC. The life of the Yellow Emperor goes back roughly one thousand years before that. For the thousands of years after his death, no matter how dynasties came and went, the status of the Yellow Emperor as the ancestor of the Chinese people has never wavered. Paying respects by making sacrifices or offerings to the Yellow Emperor became one of the necessary rites of every successive head of a dynasty. The Yellow Emperor's Tomb became a symbol, strengthening the solidarity of the tribe, honoring

the ancestors, serving as a locus of respect and belonging. On the eve of the irruption of the War of Resistance against Japan, in the midst of efforts to save the Chinese people representatives were sent from both parties of China to the Xuanyuan Tomb. These two parties held different political views, but they came to commemorate the great ancestor of all Chinese people and to carry out official rites at the time of the Pure Brightness Festival in 1937.

Memorial postal articles that reflect the life and achievements of the Yellow Emperor in the year 2007.

From 1955 to 1962, offering rites were carried out every year by Shaanxi Province at the time of the Pure Brightness Festival, but these activities were stopped in 1963 and not resumed until 1980. Since then, they have been held every year in a formal and impressive way, officiated by the National People's Congress and the CPPCC. In 1992, Shaanxi Province began repairs of the Yellow Emperor Tomb. Today, commemorating the Yellow Emperor with public offerings has become a kind of expression of the cohesiveness of the Chinese people. Many overseas Chinese and compatriots from Hong Kong, Macao, and Taiwan come to participate, and one can see that there is no substitute for the position of the Yellow Emperor in the hearts and minds of his "sons and grandsons."

The Yin Ruins and the Origin of Chinese Characters

Among all the letter systems worldwide, the Chinese character is very unique and generates great interest. Let's go visit the origin of Chinese characters, the Yin Ruins. The Yin Ruins is the relics that the capital of the Shang Dynasty left, located around Xiaotun Village 25 kilometers northwest of Anyang, Henan. During the 14th century BC, the tenth king of Shang, Pan Geng, moved the

The bone and shell relics of the Yin Ruins excavated in 1899.

capital from Yan of Shangdong to Yin. Historians call this period the Yin-Shang Dynasty, which became the political, economic, and cultural center of that time. During the 11th century BC, the son of Diyi succeeded the throne and became King Zhou. He was a notorious tyrant in history that doted on Daji, his beautiful concubine, and cruelly treated his ministers and people. His violent reign led to mass betrayal. The Zhou Tribe, located in today's Shaanxi, aligned the leuds and crusaded against King Zhou, who was defeated at Muye and burned himself at Lutai terrace. The Yin-Shang Dynasty thus passed eight generations with ten kings and ruled for 273 years. After Zhou took over Yin-Shang, the prosperous royal capital around Xiaotun gradually declined. The Yin-Shang civilization had been buried and become the Yin Ruins.

Three thousand years passed. At the end of the 19th century, the peasants in Xiaotun often found pieces of bones during cultivation. Some of them have carvings on surface so they call them "dragon bones" and sold them to pharmacies to treat malaria and wounds. Antique traders sold them as rare medicines to a pharmacy in

The discoverer of the bone and shell relics, Wang Yirong.

A corner of the Museum of the Yin Ruins.

Beijing, the Darentang Pharmacy at Caishikou in Beijing. The "dragon bones" were encountered by epigraphy expert Wang Yirong. Wang Yirong was suffering from malaria then and went to get some Chinese medicine. When he checked the medicine, he was surprised by the carvings on the "dragon bones," in shapes of human and animals. After careful examination, he realized that they are image characters of the ancient times. The carvings recorded the names of the Shang Emperors, so he realized that they are bones for augury in Shang. Along with ancient writing expert Luo Zhenyu and writer Liu E, he traced the origin and found the antique trader who transported these "dragon bones." The trader cheated him and said the bones were from Tangyin of Henan. Wang Yirong purchased a thousand pieces of bones with a high price, but did not obtain the information on the real location of the dragon bones. Luo Zhenyu bribed out the real location of the dragon bones and continued with

Stele woods of the bone and shell in the Museum of the Yin Ruins.

further research. The discovery of inscriptions on bones and tortoise shells became great news for archaeology. The Yin Ruins began to attract great attention worldwide. The description of the Shang Dynasty in *Shi Ji* (*Historical Records*) by Sima Qian can be testified. It's very regretful that after one year of research, Wang Yirong went to war against the aggression of the aligned troops of eight Western nations. The Chinese were defeated and Wang Yirong committed suicide with his wife.

From 1928 to 1937, China organized 15 excavations at the Yin Ruins. War between China and Japan broke again. The Japanese aggressors came to Yin Ruins for excavations and transported relics. After 1949, archaeological activities began to be organized by the Chinese government. For eighty years since its discovery, the Yin Ruins has been excavated and archives have been opened. The structure and statistics of the Yin Ruins gradually became clarified to us. The total area of the Yin

Ruins is 30 square kilometers. There are more than 50 relics of palaces, temples, and other architectural clusters. There are 12 royal mausoleums, several thousand graves for the noble and common people, 1,000 sacrificial pits, 1,700 some moat ditches, 5 handicraft workshops, 160 thousand pieces of bones, with a total number of 1.6 million words and 4,500 characters, 1,700 of them can be recognized as Chinese characters. There are also quantities of bronze wares, jade wares, ceramic wares, and bone wares. The world of history and archaeology was overwhelmed.

The inscriptions on bones and tortoise shells of the Yin Ruins are among the most important archaeological discoveries of the Shang Dynasty. The collection, compilation, decoding, and study of these inscriptions over the past century have born fruitful achievements. The inscriptions are proven to be a relatively mature letter system, a stage

A rather intact piece of bone.

甲	乙	丙	丁	戊	己	庚	辛	壬	癸
虎	马	鹿	牛	兕	羊	象	鱼	鹏	蚕
雷	雨	水	虹	日	月	夕	车	土	王
并	闻	伐	获	降	射	身	渔	坠	易

Comparison table of some of the inscriptions on bones and tortoise shells with the modern Chinese characters.

in the legend of Cang Jie's invention of the Chinese characters. The Chinese written language, with the jumping-off point of these inscriptions, is a letter system of hieroglyphic characters. It differs much from today's universal spelling letters. It has gone through inscriptions on bronze, bamboo slips, and developed to written characters on paper. It has formed different fonts like regular script, running script, official script, cursive style, etc. And it also brought into being the art of Chinese calligraphy. China is a country with a vast territory and various ethnic groups and dialects. The Chinese written language has been functioning greatly to the unification of the country and

Copper *ding* vessel Si Mu Wu.

intercommunion of the people.

In 1961, the State Council listed the Yin Ruins as State Protected Cultural Relic. The main protected area includes the palaces and temples around Xiaotun Village. That used to be the heart of the Imperial Capital where the Emperor lived and dealt with administrative affairs. North to Wuguan Village at the north bank of Heng

The restored Xiang Hall of the Fuhao Grave and Fuhao Statue. The name of "Fuhao" was found in the inscriptions on bones and tortoise shells of the Wuding Period. We learnt that Fuhao used to take charge in sacrificial ceremonies and war affairs. Due to her prestiged status, she should have been the mate of Wuding.

River is where the Imperial Mausoleum located. All the Emperors after Pan Geng moved the capital to Yin lie beneath this place. This was also a grand sacrificial place that held slaughterings for ancestor worship rituals.

In July 2006, UNESCO listed the Yin Ruins as a World Heritage Site.

Confucius and His Homeland

During the Spring and Autumn Period (770–476 BC) and the Warring States Period (475–221 BC), philolophy and culture developed to a peak in China. Various schools of ideas appeared and free arguments and competitions took place. They were later called "the hundred schools of thoughts." Among them include the Confucian School represented by Confucius, Mencius, and Xunzi; the Taoist School represented by Laozi and Zhuangzi; the Mohist School represented by Mozi; the School of Legalists represented by Han Fei and Shang Yang; the School of Logicians represented by Gongsun Long and Hui Shi; the Yin-Yang School represented by Zou Yan; and the School of Political Strategists represented by Su Qin and Zhang Yi; etc. Confucius and the Confucian School had the greatest impact in Chinese history.

The portrait of Confucius by Ma Yuan.

Confucius is a philosopher, politician, educator, and the founder of the Confucian School during the latter years of the Spring and Autumn Period. He is regarded as a world-class giant with Jesus, Socrates, Mohammed the Prophet, and Sakyamuni the Buddha. Confucius was born in the state of Lu (today's Qufu in Shangdong Province). At the age of 30, he took in disciples to spread his doctrines and ideas. At the age of 31, he assumed the office of attorney generalin Lu. Later on, he resigned and toured Wei, Song, Cao, Chen, Cai, and other states with dozens of

A bird's eye view of the Confucian Temple.

his disciples. He aimed to persuade the monarchs with his political ideas, but in vain. For fourteen years, he had drifted from place to place, undergone hardships, misunderstanding, and disappointments. He came back to his own country in his later years, mainly engaging in education and literature compilation. He compiled the *Book of Songs, Shang Shu* (the Ancient Book), and he edited the first chronicle history in China, *Spring and Autumn*. Confucius advocated the spirit of "education for all," aiming to spread knowledge, ideas, and moral lessons to ordinary people's children. His disciples exceed three thousand in number, among which 72 became outstanding including Zilu, Yan Hui, Zeng Shen, Zigong, etc. The core of the Confucian philosophy is Ren, meaning love, tolerance, honesty, integrity, and responsibility. The Confucian philosophy is both profound and modest. His diciples had gathered and compiled his words and deeds into the Analects, which became the most important work among the "four classics" for the Chinese.

During the time when Confucius lived, China was split into dozens of independent states. Although they all regard the King of Zhou as the nominal overlord, they are independent political entities themselves. The states

Dacheng Palace of the Confucian Temple.

not only commuted and competed with each other, but also warred and annexed against each other. People suffer from the pain of war constantly. The Spring and Autumn Period started when King Ping moved the capital east to Luoyang. The royal power began to decline from then on. The states competed for domination. Annexations were frequent and political order was shattered. At the beginning of the Spring and Autumn Period, there were more than a hundred states, famous among them include Qi, Jin, Chu, Qin, Lu, Song, Wei, Yan, Chen, Cao, Cai, Zheng, Wu, Yue, etc. The Spring and Autumn Period was named after a historic work compiled by Confucius. Confucius compiled and edited the work *Spring and Autumn* by the historians of Lu. It recorded from 722 to 481 BC. It's the earliest chronological history in China. On the surface *Spring and Autumn* is an objective record of history without comments, nevertheless the words conveyed appraisal and debasement, which is called the *Spring and Autumn* style. There are three works that interpret *Spring and Autumn*, and they are *Zuo's Spring and Autumn*, *Gongyang's Spring and Autumn*, and *Guliang's Spring and Autumn*. The Spring and Autumn Period refers

The apricot altar in the Confucian Temple, where Confucius used to teach.

to the several hundred years that Confucius' *Spring and Autumn* recorded. During that period of time, economy developed and culture flourished. Ideas were relatively at liberty. Schools of thoughts appeared and were actively debating. The order and etiquette of slavery were undergoing decadence. It was a time of war and chaos. Confucius aimed to restore the harmony of Western Zhou (1046–771 BC), when a rigid system of regulations and etiquettes was maintained. Confucius advocated that system and found selfish motives and lust for power of people, especially of the kings, were the major obstacles that destroyed the system. So he called for restraint of self and desire, and aimed to restore the shattered system. In order to fulfill this aim, one must engage his behavior and mind to benevolence. Confucius advocated the obedient relationship between the king and the subject, the father and the son. He claimed that governors be concerned about his people and not generate conflicts. He claimed that people obey the laws and regulations, be responsible to his job and position, and live in harmony. The core of the Confucian philosophy is "benevolence," which is his deep understanding of humanity. The Confucian doctrine

The Confucian Woods.

was widely spread and the Confucian school gradually formed based on the *Analects*. His ideas have brought profound influence and served as the main political groundwork for the ruling class and the most powerful belief system in China for two thousand years. Prime Minister Zhao Pu of the Northern Song Dynasty (960–1127) once said that half of the *Analects'* content is enough reference to abide by for a ruler to rule the country.

During his life time, Confucius never imagined that his ideas can have such a profound impact on the Chinese political, social, and cultural lives. The Emperors of the following dynasties all paid homage to him and bestowed great honor and privilege to him as a saint. The excessive homage appears inconsistent with the difficult life Confucius led and his qualities of modesty and diligence. Nevertheless, it helped the persistent spreading of the Confucian ideas. Qufu of Shandong is the homeland of Confucius. The Confucian temple, family seat, and woods have been recorded into the World Heritages of Cultural Relics. When you walk into Qufu, you can feel history and culture in the wind. Everything here has a taste of the Confucian spirit.

The kiosk of imperial steles, totally 13 in number, with 55 steles recording the memorial ceremonies, the mending of the temple, and visiting ceremonies of the emperors in the following dynasties.

The resident houses of the Confucian Temple.

The Confucian Temple is located in the city of Qufu. The architectural structure is grand and magnificent and is the place for worshipping the saint. For 2,400 years, the worshipping of Confucius has never been interrupted. The temple is also the most ancient architectural cluster that still exists in China. There are nine connected yards, 54 gatehouses, 13 kiosks of imperial steles. The most important architecture in the Confucian Temple is the Dacheng Palace, which is the main worshipping place. The palace is magnificent and fancily decorated with dragon sculptured pillars. The Confucius statue is at the central position. On both sides are statues of successors Zengzi, Yanzi, Zisi, and Mencius, and twelve major deciples. There is a square kiosk with apricot altar in front of the palace. It is said that Confucius used to teach at this spot and the giant tree was originally planted by Confucius.

The Confucian Family Seat is at the east of the Confucian Temple. It is where the offspings of Confucius have been residing and the second most grand architectural cluster in China following the Forbidden City. The Seat has an area of 246 acres and was built into three sections, the central, east, and west part. The east section is the family temple. The west section is the school. The central section is a theme architecture.

The Confucian Woods is the city of the dead for the Confucian family. It is located at the north of Qufu and has an area of 3,000 acres. The age-old trees and steles form a forest that makes visitors feel deep esteem and sublimity.

The *Art of War* by Sunzi: A Classic on Military Theory

The *Art of War* is the ultimate gem in the legacy of China's military tradition. It is a book whose contents are profound, whose narration is comprehensive, and whose logic is tightly constructed. The author Sun Wu lived during the latter period of the Spring and Autumn Period. (The name Sunzi includes the honorific, and means Master Sun.) Sun grew up in a military family, his courtesy name was Changqing, and he was originally from the state of Qi. He was both a military theorist and a practitioner of war. Carrying his thirteen treatises on the *Art of War*, he is said to have had an audience with the King of the state of Wu, Helü, around 512 BC. At the time, the state of Chu had invaded and carved up the state of Cai. Sun Wu was there to ask for assistance from the state of Wu. The King of Wu promptly appointed Sun Wu general and Sun Wu then led the Wu armies in successful attack against the state of Chu. Sun Wu also led armies to attack two countries who would not submit to the authority of the state of Wu, called Xu and Zhongwu. His victories lend credence to the belief that Sun Wu's military theories are not the result of mere thinking, not just so-called "talking of soldiers on paper," but the result of actual battle experience. The illustrious military mastermind Sun Wu appears to have been killed in

The statue of Sun Wu.

battle in 484 BC.

The *Art of War* is divided into thirteen chapters. These include essays on Strategy, Making war, Planning attack, Appearances, Actual power or force, False or true: the real situation, Military engagement, Nine transformations, Marching the army, Topography, Nine situations on the ground, Fire attack, and Using spies. These fully cover the theory and practice of the arts of war. The book regards military affairs as being a major consideration to a country. It encourages "knowing yourself and knowing the other, for then you will not be defeated once in one hundred battles." It stresses understanding all circumstances, having a full analysis of relations with the enemy, of public actions and solo operations, of strengths and weaknesses, of trues and falses or appearances and reality, of attacking and defending, advancing and retreating, all of the contradictory aspects of the two sides to each consideration. Moreover, it assures that by understanding the objective laws of warfare and managing or controlling these laws, one is assured of victory.

"Soldiers have no constant unchanging nature just as water has no constant unchanging shape," the *Art of War* advises. "Water can modify depending on

Copper sword of Fuchai, the lord of Wu.

Copper spear excavated at Qin Emperor's Mausoleum.

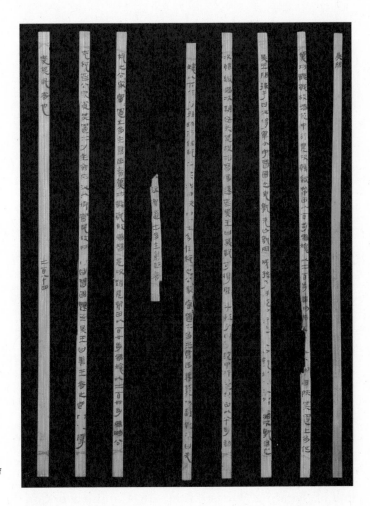

Bamboo slips of the
Art of War excavated
at Yinque Mountain of
Linyi, Shandong.

the adversary it meets up against, and win over it. This is called 'shen' or being possessed of a godlike nature. Strategic warfare emphasizes the concurrent promotion of the anomalous and the proper or common, in order to keep an advsary off balance." During the Spring and Autumn Period of history in China "one hundred schools were contending," and it was under this stimulating environment that this effective military treatise was born. The book's contents are encyclopedic. They distill the experience and the intelligence of an untold number of people from the period. Sun Wu was the most outstanding representative of an outstanding group of people. As the military scholar Mao Yuanyi said at the

The "Number One Sword" in the city of the *Art of War* in Binzhou, Shandong. Two swords intersect with each other and stand on the ground, representing peace and ceasing the war.

end of the Ming Dynasty (1368–1644) in his work on military preparedness, "Sunzi did not owe anything to those who came before him; whereas those who came after Sunzi could not omit Sunzi in their recognition of who made them."

The appearance of the *Art of War* had a profound influence on the later development of China's ancient military arts. It has been revered as the Bible of Military Affairs, the classic for all ages. Among generations of military strategists, not one does not take nourishment from this book and use it in the actual practice of war. The famous politician and military man during the Three Kingdoms period (220–265), Cao Cao, was the first to do a systematic annotation of the *Art of War*, which made the book considerably easier to use for those who came later. The *Art of War* is not merely a treasury of strategy for China, but has been famous throughout the world. It was transmitted into Japan in the 8th century and into Europe in the 18th century. It has been translated into 29 languages, and is widely read throughout the world.

The book is unlike the usual commentary or narrative. Its contents often touch upon meteorology, geography, and all kinds of specific knowledge that affects the conduct of war. The book is not something that the common man of letters could write. It is also not the reflection of life at one particular time, but rather a summary of experience over time. It is clearly the creation of a number of military experts who were versed in both letters and history. Even someone with the best background in martial and literary arts would find it impossible to write this book alone. The philosophy reflected in its military affairs comes from the distillation of the actual experience of battle. The philosophy expressed has been through the perfecting and editing of several generations, and to a certain degree one could say that the book could not have been accomplished but for the complex social background and historical circumstances of the Spring and Autumn and Warring States periods. It may well therefore not have been the work of one man, and it cannot have been the work of one short time. The great military theorist Sun Wu undoubtedly played an important role in the process of making sure that the ideas expressed in the book were put down for later generations. We are indebted to him for the *Art of War*.

Sanxingdui, a Civilization Independent from the Central Plains

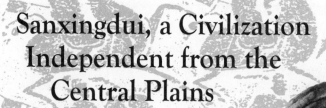

S anxingdui Site is the ruins of the Bronze Age in the southwest part of China. The location is Nanxing Town of Guanghan, Sichuan. Around 4 kilometers away from Guanghan, three loessial hills abruptly sit on the Sichuan plain. The name of Sanxingdui (Three Star Hills) got its name from its appearance. In the spring of 1929, a peasant named Yan Daocheng found a pit of fancy jade utensils while digging ditches near his house. This led to the discovery of Sanxingdui civilization. Since 1931, sacrificial ditches were frequently discovered, with jade and bronze utensils inside.

The excavation started from 1980. The relic of a town was discovered. Research found the age of the town to be early Shang Dynasty. The length of the east wall of the town is 1,100 meters, the south wall measured to 180 meters, and the west wall measured to 600 meters. All of the walls were built by hand. Later, bases of houses, ash pits, mausoleums, and sacrificial pits were discovered. The forms of the bases of houses include round, square, and rectangle. The houses were mostly wood architectures above the ground. In 1986, two huge sacrificial pits were discovered, and many bronze wares, jade statues, ivory, shells, ceramics, and gold wares were excavated. The time of the sacrificial pits is estimated to be at the end of Shang and beginning of Zhou. The pits are the relics of Sichuan people worshipping all the gods of nature. The discovery of Sanxingdui

The grand bronze statue.

The Sanxingdui Museum.

was dynamic news worldwide and is regarded as the "ninth miracle" on the globe.

The discovery of Sanxingdui dates the history of the country of Shu to 5,000 years ago. It was a relatively independent cultural system apart from the central area. The discovery validates the authenticity of the recordation of ancient Shu in literature. In the past, people assumed that ancient Shu is a relatively isolated place, with no attachment or little communication with the central state. However, the discovery of the Sanxingdui Site argues otherwise. Shu should have been an important prince state during the Shang and Zhou periods. Although its culture is unique, it still has the same origin with the culture of the central state. The Sanxingdui Site becomes a significant approach when we want to understand the historical and cultural development of Sichuan and even the southwest area.

Where did Sanxingdui culture come from? The numerous bronze figures and animal figures don't belong to any category of the bronze ware of the central state.

Bronze head, excavated from No. 2 pit.

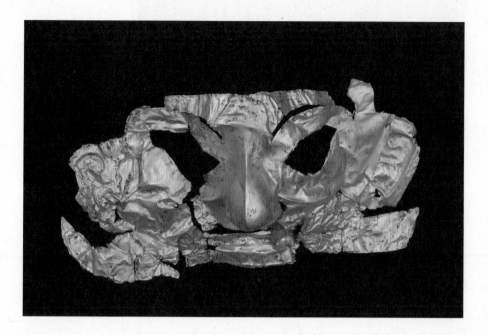

Gold mask from No. 1 pit, made by beating gold foil, with a protruding nose.

It's inconceivable that not a word was left on the bronze wares. The excavated Sanxingdui figures don't look like Chinese but rather like "foreigners" with high noses, big eyes, extruding cheekbones, wide mouths, big ears, and holes in the ears. The head of Sanxingdui workstation of Sichuan Cultural Relic and Archaeology Institution, Mr. Chen De'an, thinks that Sanxingdui people might have come from other continents and Sanxingdui civilization might be a "mixed civilization."

The prosperity of ancient Shu lasted over 1,500 years and it suddenly disappeared like when it suddenly appeared. When history is recorded again, there is a mysterious gap of over 2,000 years. There are many assumptions on the perdition of ancient Shu, but all of them lack enough evidence and stay assumptions. First there is the flood assumption. The north of Sanxindui Site lies the Yazi River, and Mamu River flows through the city. Thus some scholars think that the civilization was destroyed by the flood. However, achaeologists have not found sediment layers left by floods at the site. Then there is the war assumption. The utensils and wares in the site were destroyed or burnt prior to excavation and this

Copper bird.

seems to confirm this explanation. But later it was found that these wares are from different times over hundreds of years. And there is the migration assumption which does not need too much research. But this assumption does not explain the reason people migrate. Chengdu Plain is rich with good soil and various products. The weather is also mild. It's hard to justify the calamity assumption and the real reason for the disappearance of ancient Shu in history is still a myth. The continued discovery of Jinsha Site in 2001 after Sanxingdui might provide a persuasive reference to the myth of Sanxingdui civilization. As experts speculate, Jinsha is the new political center of ancient Shu state after San Xingdui. The Jinsha civilization existed from the later years of the Shang Dynasty to the early years of the Spring and Authumn Period (c. 1200 –650 BC). In 316 BC, two regimes in Suchuan, Ba and Shu, were destroyed

Sea shell unearthed in Sanxingdui Site.

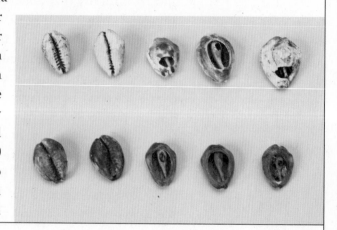

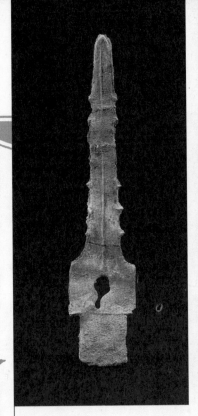

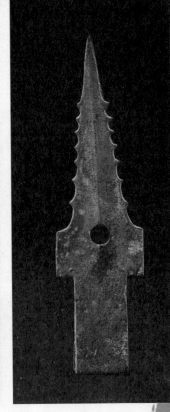

Copper dagger. It served most likely as a ceremonial staff in religious affairs rather than a weapon.

by Qin. The ancient Shu civilization started to blend gradually into the Chinese civilization from then.

Among the numerous bronze wares excavated from Sanxingdui, there are seldom daily utensils. The majority is articles for sacrifice. This indicates that the ancient religious system in Shu is already mature. These articles have their unique cultural characteristics and the bronze statues and gold staffs are very close to those of Maya and Egyptian civilizations in form. The deputy curator of Sanxingdui Museum, Mr. Zhang Jizhong, claims that Sanxingdui might have been the center of world pilgrimage due to the numerous sacrificial articles from different regions. Over 5,000 shells were excavated from the pit and were identified to have come from the Indian Ocean. Some scholars think these shells were early foreign exchange currency for trade in Sichuan, while others think they are sacrificial articles brought by pilgrims. It would be an inconceivable phenomenon if the assumed isolated Shu had "foreign investments" then.

An invaluable treasure was discovered from the sacrificial pit and it's the earliest gold staff in the world. The explanation of its use as a royal staff is already

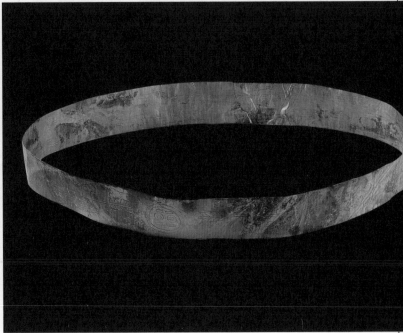

agreed by the academic circle, but the inscribed fish and arrows on it generated lots of arguments. Sanxingdui has already possessed the necessary factors of civilization, lacking only written language. Argument on this issue has a long history. The *Biography of Lord Shu* recorded that ancient Shu people "did not have any written language and thus did not have ceremonial music." The *History of Huayang State* says that the Shu people "are rich with good writings." Whether the inscriptions on the gold staff are pictures or letters, there is no agreement yet. Some scholars are aiming at deciphering them, others regard the symbols as individual existence and not expressive language. If these pictures can be deciphered, the myth of Sanxingdui will be solved to a great extent. Whether Sanxingdui had written language or not remains to be a myth.

The gold stick unearthed in Sanxingdui Site and the gold crown band unearthed in Jinsha Site. Both of them have the combined designs of man heads, arrows, birds, and fish. They bear an almost same style, which shows the continuity of the Jinsha culture and the Sanxingdui culture.

The Qin Mausoleum and the Terracotta Warriors: the Rise and Fall of the Qin Empire

The mausoleum of the Qin Emperor is located at the foot of Li Mountains east of Lintong town, around 30 kilometers from the city of Xi'an. Qin Emperor Ying Zheng is a hero of great talent and bold vision. During the war between the seven states, he developed economy and military forces internally, while advocating inter-states alliance externally. After bloody conquests, Qin (221–206 BC) destroyed the other six states and established a unified and centralized empire. He unified the law system, the measure system, the coin system, and the language. He organized road construction and established the county system, which contributed to the unification and economic development of China. On the other hand, he was extremely dominating and violent. He regarded the people as of no importance and the state as his own wealth. He extorted excessive taxes and levies, carried out severe criminal penalty laws, led excessively luxurious

Sketch map of the unified coin. After the Qin Emperor unified the other six states, he changed the cloth coin, the knife coin, the round coin, and the copper shell to a round coin with a square hole inside.

life, not to mention that he burned books and buried scholars. During his reign, the governance is already under great danger as the people suffer from misery and conflicts intensified. After his death, his fatuous and weak son succeeded the throne and became the puppet of the guile and atrocious eunuchs. The political and economic situation was getting geopardized. Finally, the uprising of Chen Sheng and Wu Guang broke out and it led to many responses from the opposing forces. The short-lived dynasty was thus overthrown. The Qin mausoleum began to construct when the Emperor was 13 years old. The Prime Minister Li Si organized the planning and designing. General Zhang Han supervised the engineering process, which took 38 years. The project exceeded all of the rulers' mausoleums in scale and luxury. The population of Qin was around 20 million, and 720 thousand men underwent the servitude of building the mausoleum.

The height of the Qin Mausoleum is 43 meters, with the base perimeter of more than 1,700 meters. There are two layers of clay city wall. The interior city is in square shape with a perimeter of 3,890 meters. There are two doors on the north side and one door for each of the other three sides. The exterior city is in the shape of rectangle with a perimeter of 6,294 meters. There is a door on

View of the earth grave of the mausoleum of Qin Emperor from afar.

each side. The mausoleum is located at the south of the cemetery.

The terracotta warrior pits accompany the mausoleum of the Qin Emperor. It is located 1,500 meters east of the cemetery. For some years, this used to be a grave yard. The peasants have found figures like real persons when they dig up the graves. In March 1974, the village peasants at the east of the cemetery digged wells for water and incidentally discovered the grand pit of terracotta warriors. After achaeologists' excavation, the precious deposits of the terracottà warriors over 2,000 years are finally uncovered. The three terracotta warrior pits lie from west to east. The number one pit which was discovered first is in the shape of a rectangle. The length is 230 meters, the width is 62 meters, and the deepness is around 5 meters, with an area of 14,260 square meters. There are ramp gateways to all four directions. To each of its side there are the number two pit and number three pit.

The terracotta warrior pit is the largest scale

underground military museum in the whole world. The composition of the pits is well arranged and the structure is unique. At the bottom of the pit, a main wall is built from west to east every other 3 meters and the terracotta warriors are disposed between the walls. 500 warriors are excavated in pit number one, among 6 chariots, 24 vehicle horses, and bronze and iron weapons such as bronze swords, Wu swords, spears, arrows, crossbows, halberds, etc. There are 210 life size terracotta warriors at the east of the pit, with various expressions, garments, and hair styles. Each of them is lively and vivid, including generals, pommel horses, shoot warriors in kneeling position, etc. They line in three horizontal processions, 70 in each. The three leaders wear armors and the rest of the troops wear short clothes with leggings and hairdo without helmets. All of them have bows and arrows and crossbows, appearing to be awaiting orders to depart as vanguard armies. Following behind is the main troop

No. 1 pit of the terracotta warriors.

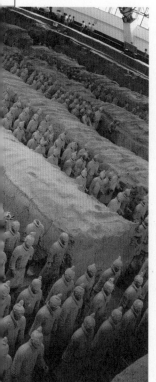

consisting of 6,000 armored warriors, each with three meter long weapons like spears, daggers, or harberds. Together in the pit are 35 chariots with four horses in 11 passages, lining in 38 columns. The vigour of the terracotta warriors is the artistic representation of the Qin Emperor's mighty armies when he destroyed the other six states and united China.

The Qin Mausoleum is an architecture that the Qin Emperor built for his eternal blessedness. He spent the major portion of the country's labor and resources. However, the wisdom and craftiness of the erectors have been highly represented in this great piece of architectural art. Modern visitors admire the ancient artisans' creation, at the same time abhor the violence of the Qin Emperor. After the Qin Emperor's death, his son Qin Junior carried over the construction of the mausoleum and the warrior pits. This further aggravated people's burden. Before the construction of the mausoleum is finished, peasant uprising lead by Chen Sheng and Wu Guang broke

No. 1 copper vehicle and horse.

out. The joint force of Xiang Yu and Liu Bang finally overthrew the Qin Dynasty. Pit number three was not finished and pit number four did not have the chance to put terracotta warriors inside, and they were filled up in haste with the entire project unfinished.

The Qin Mausoleum is the largest in scale, oddest in structure, and richest in connotation among mausoleums of kings and emperors all over the world. It is actually a luxurious underground palace. International leaders and scholars come to visit the terracotta warrior museum and regard the discovery of the pits as a significant discovery in archaeology and the eighth miracle in the world. It can be compared with the Egyptian pyramids and the Greek sculptures.

In 1961, the State Department of China nominated

Tomb figure of a high rank soldier; head of a general; various kinds of terracotta warriors. The "eternal charm" of the terracotta warriors rests in the creation of life size Qin figures of thousands of different status, personalities, and spirits.

the Qin Mausoleum to be a national protected institution. In 1987, UNESCO approved the Qin Mausoleum and the terracotta warrior pits to join the World Heritage list. A vaulted exhibition hall was built above the No. 1 warrior pit. The Museum of Qin Mausoleum and the warrior pits are open to tourists.

Restored warrior from excavation.

The Graves of Huo Qubing and Wang Zhaojun

The Huns is an ancient nomad tribe in North China. At the end of the Warring States Period, the Huns annoyed the northern territory of Qin, Zhao, and Yan. The three states thus started to build the Great Wall to resist the Huns. Chief Modu (ruled from 209–174 BC) united the tribes and established the state which territory covers the vast area north and south of the Gobi desert. Thenceforth, the Huns extended its territory east to the Liao River, west over the Pamirs, north to Baikal Lake, and south almost to the Great Wall. It has become the first grassland nomad empire in history. At the beginning of Western Han (206 BC–25 AD), the Huns continued to harry the south. In 200 BC, they surrounded Emperor Gaozu of Han, Liu Bang, at Mount Baideng (northeast of Datong, Shanxi) and forced the Han Dynasty to carry out peaceful policies, to pay intribute annually, and to open up market with them for trade. However, the Huns

Grave of Huo Qubing.

Jiuquan Park in Jiuquan, Gansu. The park got its name from a wine fountain. It is recorded in history that in 121 BC during the Han Dynasty, Piaoqi General Huo Qubing conquered the Huns in the west and achieved great victory. Emperor Wu awarded him the imperial wine. Huo Qubing credited the victory to the whole army and poured the wine into the fountain to share with all the soldiers. The fountain was named wine fountain ever since.

frequently broke their agreement and invade the south. The Huns had become a great frontier trouble of the Han Dynasty. During the reign of Emperor Wudi, the state power of Western Han became strong and sent troops to beat back the Huns for three times (127 BC, 121 BC, 119 BC). The power of the Huns gradually declined.

At the beginning of Eastern Han (25–220), the Huns broke up to the north and south parts. King Rizhu led over 400,000 soldiers down south to attach to the Han Dynasty. They were named South Hun and were allocated by the Han at the Hetao area. The Huns remained at the north was named the North Hun. From 89 to 91 AD, the South Hun and the Han allied their troops to attack the North Hun. The latter was beaten twice at the north of the desert and the Altai Mountains. The North Huns was forced to retrieve to the west and disappeared from Chinese history forever. Most scholars take the Huns in European history to be the North Huns that moved west.

During the lasting war between China and the Huns, two historic figures were recorded and remembered. They are Huo Qubing and Wang Zhaojun.

Huo Qubing (140–117 BC) was a famous general during the reign of Emperor Wu. He had established his battle achievements in the wars with the Huns. Huo was the nephew of General Wei Qing. His mother, Wei Shao'er, was a sister of Empress Wei Zifu. Huo Qubing was adept at cavalry and toxophily. In 123 BC, Huo followed General Wei Qing to the north to conquer the Huns. He led 800 elite cavalry soldiers and chased the Huns for hundreds of kilometers. 2,028 Hun soldiers were killed in that battle, including the chief's grandfather. They also caught the chief's uncle. Huo was homaged as the "Champion Marquis."

In 121 BC, Huo Qubing was promoted to the position of Piaoqi General and led 10,000 cavalry soldiers to go out of Longxi and thousands of kilometers over the Yanzhi Mountain (south of Shandan, Gansu). He killed Zhelan Chief of the Huns, caught the son of Hunxie Chief, and annihilated 8,000 Hun soldiers. In the summer of 121 BC, Huo Qubing went out of Longxi again over 2,500 kilometers beyond Juyanze, He caught Chief Qiutu at Qilian Mountain and killed over 30,000 soidiers and accepted surrender of 2,500 soldiers, while his own troops lost less than one third in number. This battle was a heavy blow upon the Huns.

"Horse stepping on the Hun": a horse stands firmly with its head up, underneath its hoof lies a Hun aristocrat. This is a stone statue that the Emperor Wu of Han ordered to be made in memorial of Huo Qubing. It stands in front of the grave of Huo Qubing.

In the autumn of the same year, the Hun chief got angry at the failures and losses of Chief Hunye's battles and had the plan to kill Chief Hunye in his fury. Chief Hunye suggested surrender to the Han Dynasty to Chief Xiutu. Emperor Wu was suspicious about their surrender and sent Huo Qubing to receive them with his troops. Huo Qubing crossed the Yellow River and approached Chief Hunye's army. But some of Chief Hunye's followers changed their mind when they saw the Han troops and escaped in disorder. Huo Qubing rushed to the camp of Chief Hunye and discussed with him. They killed the 8,000 soldiers that didn't want to surrender and finally, Chief Hunye led 40,000 soldiers and pledged allegiance to the Han Dynasty. The successful surrender ensured the longterm peace and stability of the Hexi region, and Han thus got through the path to the western territories. In 117 BC, Emperor Wu took advantage of the Huns' assumption that Han dared not go into the desert for war. He sent Wei Qing and Huo Qubing to attack the Huns respectively, each with 50,000 cavalry, 40,000 equipped horses, and hundreds of thousands of soldiers and supplying troops. Huo Qubing set off from Dai Prefecture and caught Chief Tuntou, Chief Han, and 83 followers. His troops killed more than 70,000 soldiers. Huo Qubing was thus promoted to Grand Sima Piaoqi General. Emperor Wudi regarded highly of Huo Qubing and once proposed to build a luxurious house for him. However, Huo Qubing answered, "The Huns are not annihilated completely, what do I need a house for?" This saying became a motto for generals and patriots throughout the dynasties for expressing lofty sentiments. In 117 BC, Huo Qubing died of illness at the age of 23. Emperor Wu grieved heavily and ordered to bury him at Mao Mausoleum (Emperor Wu's own mausoleum in Xingping County at the northwest of Xi'an, Shaanxi). Emperor Wu built his grave in the shape of Qilian Mountain, symbolizing the battle field that Huo Qubing had fought.

There are 16 stone sculptures at the front of Huo Qubing's grave, including stone figures, stone horses, and other various topics. The style of the sculptures is simple and rough. They are so far the most ancient and best preserved great sculpture artworks in China and are of great significance in Chinese art history.

Wang Zhaojun (52–19 BC), whose first name was Qiang, was born in Baoping Village of Xingshan County in Hubei Province. She was selected into the imperial palace during Emperor Yuan's reign in Western Han, but she was ignored for many years. In 33 BC, Chief

Huhanye of the Huns entered into the imperial palace and expressed that he would like to marry a Chinese girl for his wife. Zhaojun volunteered to marry the chief. Before departure, Emperor Yuan discovered her uncommon beauty and regretted about his decision. However, he could not change his mind in order to earn the Huns' trust. He reluctantly sent Zhaojun to marry Chief Huhanye. In remembrance of Zhaojun's departure abroad, Emperor Yuan changed the name of the year to "Jingning," meaning peaceful frontier. Chief Huhanye made Zhaojun his wife name "Ninghu Yanzhi." People call Zhaojun "peaceful emissary" in history.

The grave of Zhaojun is located at the bank of Dahei River in the south suburb of Hohhot, Inner Mongolia. Both historic record and folk legend regard it as the grave of Wang Zhaojun over 2,000 years from now. It is a key relic site in Inner Mongolia today. The height of the grave is 33 meters, with a bottom area of 13,000 square meters. It is among the biggest Han graves in China. Since

Painting of *Mingfei Going North* by Gong Suran.

Sculpture in memory of the intermarriage of the Huns and
Han in front of the grave of Zhaojun.

"Green tomb": the grave of Zhaojun.

Zhaojun's grave has been covered with green grass, it also has the name of "Green Grave." From a distance, the Green Grave stands by itself and appears like a Chinese painting. The site had become one of Hohhot's Eight Landscapes.

Zhaojun's homeland: Memorial Museum of Zhaojun in Baoping Village of Xingshan, Hubei.

In Chinese history, Wang Zhaojun is a great lady who dedicated herself to the cause of national peace. People also regard her as a symbol of womanly beauty. For thousands of years, legends and folklores about her life have been spread everywhere. After the Tang (618–907) and Song (960–1279) dynasties, scholars created poetry, songs, paintings, and dramas on Zhaojun's topic. Jian Bozan, a history scholar, summarized the Zhaojun culture as the follows, "Wang Zhaojun is not just a figure but a symbol of good will between the ethnic groups. The grave of Zhaojun is not just a grave but a cenotaph of ethnic friendship."

Romance of the Three Kingdoms: In Search of the Traces of the Heroes of the Three Kingdoms

The historical novel for which the Chinese hold greatest affection and highest regard is called the *Romance of the Three Kingdoms*. This work of the 14th century was written on the basis of an historical work called the *Records of Three Kingdoms*. This latter was the "unofficial history" of the kingdoms called Wei, Shu, and Wu when they were at their height in the period following the Han dynasty. The historical work is a magnum opus: the *Book*

The retreating place of Zhuge Liang: Longzhong in Xiangyang, Hubei.

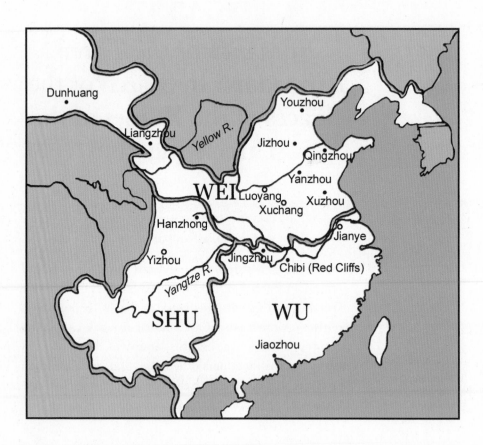

of *Wei* is 30 volumes, *Shu* is 15 volumes, and *Wu* is 20 volumes. These 65 volumes narrate a history of over sixty years, from the first year of the reign of Wei Wendi in 220 AD to the first year of the reign of Jin Wudi in 280 AD. The author of the historical work is the man Chen Shou (233–297) of early Western Jin (265–317). Chen Shou was in name writing the history of Wei, but since the Wei was concurrent with Shu and Wu, he wrote their histories as well.

Map of the Three Kingdoms.

The *Romance of the Three Kingdoms* was written much later, in the 14th century as noted above, by a man named Luo Guanzhong, but was very much based on this earlier work and also on oral tradition.

In the latter Eastern-Han period (25–220), when the political structure was increasingly corrupt, state policies were in disarray, unrest was pervasive and refugees were fleeing throughout the land, opportunities for revolt

Woodcarving of lattice for the window of the Chen family in Guangzhou: the legends of the "Three Calls at the Cottage" and the "Battle of the Red Cliffs." The culture of the Three Kingdoms had deeply rooted and blended into the Chinese traditional culture.

Exhibition Museum of the Battle of the Red Cliffs, Hubei.

became more common. One revolt took as its pretext the putting down of the Yellow Turban Army uprising (184 AD). The revolt was successful and the Eastern Han continued on in name but not in actuality. Among those military leaders who were carving off power for themselves, the strongest and most active were Cao Cao and Yuan Shao.

Cao Cao and Yuan Shao fought their final decisive battle in the year 200. In this battle, Cao Cao defeated Yuan Shao and became head of the strongest military grouping in the north. In order to continue his ambition to unify "all under heaven," in 208 he led his army southward and occupied Jingzhou, coming up against forces of Sun Quan in the lower reaches of the Yangtze River. Just at this time, the fleeing successor to the last Han throne had also raised armies and was attempting a comeback. Liu Bei and Sun joined forces to counter Cao Cao. Liu Bei dispatched his commander Zhuge Liang

Wuhou Temple in Chengdu.

Figures of the Shu state in Wuhou Temple in Chengdu.

to persuade Sun Quan and they joined in battle at the Battle of the Red Cliffs. Cao Cao was utterly defeated at this battle and retreated northward, while Liu Bei occupied Jingzhou and later entered Chengdu. In 220, Cao Cao died and his son succeeded Han Xiandi, setting up a country called Wei, also known as Cao Wei. The next year, Liu Bei was proclaimed Emperor in Chengdu with a country name of Han, also Shu Han. In 229, Wu King Sun Quan set up a country called Wu. The era of the three kingdoms officially began, with the three great powers of Cao, Sun and Liu contending for power and

Guandi Temple in Xiezhou, Shanxi.

forming the three legs of an unstable tripod. The three countries coexisted for a period of 34 years (229–263), but a situation of contending factions existed for much longer, around 90 years (190–280). Wei was the strongest of the three in terms of military power, then Wu, with Shu the weakest. Ultimately, the Jin state, which replaced Wei, was successful in uniting the three. Wu lasted longest as a state, for 52 years, then Wei, for 45 years, and then Shu, for 43 years. The Jin Emperor defeated Wu in 280 which brought the epoch of the Three Kingdoms to an end.

Although ceaseless warfare characterized the period of the Three Kingdoms, in their early periods each was intent on restoring order in society, developing their economies and restructuring political systems. Cao Wei's accomplishments were most outstanding in this regard. When he unified the north, he began a program of "*tuntian*" or having peasants and garrisoned soldiers plow up wasteland and grow food, he gradually restored production; he reformed a number of corrupt practices

Guan Yu's homeland in Changping Village of Xiezhou, Yuncheng, Shanxi.

in government and controlled the power of the large landholders. He rid the court of powerful eunuchs and broke the autocratic power of their relatives, and he absorbed lower-level landowning-class people into the ranks of government. The Prime Minister of Shu, Zhuge Liang, was known for his strict use of legalism, his discipline, his meting out of punishments and rewards. These contributed to a gradual restoration and development of Shu agriculture and light industry, and to a strengthening of regional power. Particularly as a result of campaigns to the south, national miniority areas began to be developed, and national solidarity began to strengthen. From the year 211, when Sun moved the capital of Wu and began his administration, the southeastern region developed rapidly. Land was brought under cultivation, agriculture developed, government was stable, navigation and trade grew.

The *Romance of the Three Kingdoms* is ancient China's first long novel, establishing a traditional form in which each chapter was headed by a couplet giving a preview of what was to come. It was written by Luo Guanzhong, who lived from around 1330 to1400. The novel described the political and military conflicts of the three states of Wei, Shu, and Wu, and their three leaders, Cao Cao, Liu Bei, and Sun Quan. The three states engaged in plenty of actual fighting with swords and horses, but also in intrigue and cunning, and the "lip-guns" and "tongue swords" of diplomacy at the time are the material for fantastic stories. Among the most famous is the Battle of the Red Cliffs. In addition to vivid portrayals of the three main characters, another featured personality is Zhuge Liang, with his courage, wisdom, and loyalty. He has long since become a timeless model for the ages. Other characters include the outstanding strategist Zhou Yu, the honest and righteous incarnation Guan Yu, the fearless and symbolic Zhang Fei. Chinese people are steeped in these stories and their characters; many phrases have become common sayings and entered daily Chinese usage. Zhuge Liang, Guan Yu and Zhang Fei are literary figures, but Cao Cao and Zhuge Liang also played an important role in official history. Their own poetry is extremely beautiful and has become an important legacy in the cultural inheritance of greater China.

A number of places in China are known as famous sites of the exploits of the Three Kingdoms' heroes. These include the Red Cliffs in Hubei Province, the site of Liu Bei's leavetaking from this world in Chongqing and the place in Nanjing where Sun Quan locked up Wu. Among these, the most famous and most influential are the temples in commemoration of Zhuge Liang and Guan Yu.

Wang Xizhi Playing with Geese by Southern Song artist Ma Yuan. The painting depicts Wang Xizhi sitting by a pine tree and among lotus ponds, two geese are playing in the water. Wang Xizhi loved goose. He realized the tao of calligraphy while watching geese dancing. He once wrote sutra for a Shanyin Taoist in exchange of geese.

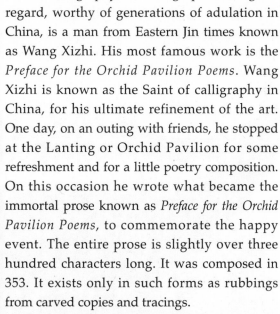

Preface for the Orchid Pavilion Poems: Social, Economic, and Cultural Lives of Wei, Jin, and the Northern and Southern Dynasties

The unique Chinese system of writing its script in characters has led to extraordinary achievements in the art of calligraphy. The calligrapher of highest regard, worthy of generations of adulation in China, is a man from Eastern Jin times known as Wang Xizhi. His most famous work is the *Preface for the Orchid Pavilion Poems*. Wang Xizhi is known as the Saint of calligraphy in China, for his ultimate refinement of the art. One day, on an outing with friends, he stopped at the Lanting or Orchid Pavilion for some refreshment and for a little poetry composition. On this occasion he wrote what became the immortal prose known as *Preface for the Orchid Pavilion Poems*, to commemorate the happy event. The entire prose is slightly over three hundred characters long. It was composed in 353. It exists only in such forms as rubbings from carved copies and tracings.

The lines have become part of the necessary education of a Chinese student, and the calligraphed beauty of the characters have become a model for generations of artists and practitioners of calligraphic arts. Although it is said that the original no longer exists, people to this day wonder if it was not buried in the Tang-dynasty tomb of Empress Wu Zetian. It is more likely that the treasure was long since swept away by the river of time.

In the year 280, as successor to the Cao Wei Kingdom, the Western Jin annihilated the Wu Kingdom. Western Jin (265–316) unified the country but only ruled in stable fashion for some twenty years before internal contradictions led to its downfall. After Western Jin was annihilated in turn, a succession of five different political powers ruled south of the Yangtze River: Eastern Jin (317–420), Song (420–479), Qi (479–502), Liang (502–557), and Chen (557–589). In the north, meanwhile, some sixteen political powers contended, including the various northern tribes of Xiongnu, Xianbi, Jie, Di, Qiang, and also Han Chinese. The period is known in history as the "Five Hu and Sixteen states (304–439)." Hu is a term applied to the five non-Han nationalities living in the northern and western part of contemporary China in ancient times. In 439, the state of Bei-Wei or Northern

Orchid Pavilion in Shaoxing, Zhejiang, located along Lanzhu Mountain, 40 kilometers southwest of Shaoxing. It used to be Wang Xizhi's residence.

Goose pond at the Orchid Pavilion site.

Wei (386–534) unified the north and continued its rule until 534. South of the river, the fragmented powers of Song, Qi, Liang, and Chen faced off against each other in a generally north-south configuration, leading to the term in history known as the Northern and Southern Dynasties period (420–589). In the year 581, the Sui (581–618) replaced a group who had already unified the northern side, known as the Northern Zhou (557–581), and in 589 it defeated the Chen and succeeded in unifying the entire country. The period known as Wei, Jin, and the Northern and Southern Dynasties or Six Dynasties came to an end.

The long period of warfare during the Wei, Jin, and the Northern and Southern Dynasties period and the bitter political infighting led many people to grow disenchanted with the prevailing Confucian philosophy of engagement with the world. They turned towards a more reclusive or escapist posture, a seeking after other-worldly enlightenment, and the rapid spread of Buddhism is evidence of this. All kinds of philosophies, arts, and different ways of thinking came into the space opened up by the turning away from previous dogma, forming a golden era of "thought liberation" not seen since the Warring States Period. Social conditions gradually moved from an era of warfare to an era of peace and stability, and the economy developed as productive forces were restored. South of the river, the swift development of agriculture

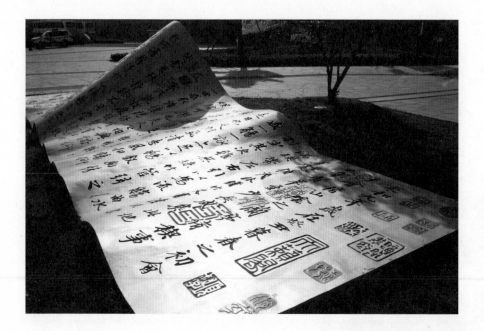

Shaoxing city sculpture: *Preface for the Orchid Pavilion Poems.*

was enhanced by changes in agricultural technology and the region gradually became the center of China's economy. In the north, the melding and coexistence of various kinds of people was helped by similar changes in agricultural technology and also by the refurbishing of canals and irrigation projects.

Arts and culture in general made long strides forward under these political and economic conditions. The literary arts of the Wei, Jin, and the Northern and Southern Dynasties were of a particular quality—the work of certain known artists shines a clear light on the spirit of humanism. These artists and their art include the poetry of Cao Zhi and Tao Yuanming, the philosophy of the so-called Seven Sages of the Bamboo Grove, the calligraphy of Wang Xizhi, the painting of Gu Kaizhi, and the proses of the Six Dynasties. Although their artistic creations often contained an underlying sense of pessimism and escapism, the weight of history cannot cover over the brilliance of their works. We see recognize the rays of light from the calligraphic work of Wang Xizhi.

Wang Xizhi lived from around 321 to 379. His

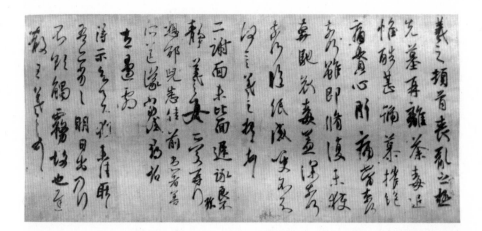

Painful Losing Note by Wang Xizhi, stored secretly in Japanese royal palace after it was brought to Japan in the Tang Dynasty. It represents the best work of Wang Xizhi's later style.

courtesy name was Yishao, and he hailed from a place that is now called Linyi in Shandong. He came from a line of illustrious and successful aristocrats. His father, grandfather, and father's elder brother were all high officials in the Eastern Jin government, elevated elite and powerful. Wang Xizhi first served as an executive, an official, and later as a military advisor before being transferred to serve in Ningyuan as General. In the end he became what is known as "Right-Army General," so that he is also referred to as Wang Right-Army. The term "right" was applied to the western flank of an army, since the perspective of the northern rulers of China at the time was that of looking southward. Hence the "right-hand" army was the army on the western side.

Wang Xizhi was known to have a very straightforward disposition, one that did not pay lip service to etiquette and formality. One citation in history refers to the story of his lying on the eastern bed with a bare chest. The story goes as follows: a notable family in the Jin Dynasty wanted to marry into the Wang family, so it sent a person over to discuss marriage with the Wang clan. The father of Wang Xizhi led this person over to gaze into the place where the sons were resting. On returning, he gave his report, saying that all the sons looked fine but one of them was lying on the eastern bed, eating something with his chest bared, as though he cared nothing about the scrutiny of the potential matchmaker. The father of the bride heard this and immediately said, "That is the one I want as my son-in-law." On later investigation, he found out that this son was Wang Xizhi, and he married his daughter to him. Since Wang Xizhi was not of high rank—the court tried many times to get him to accept various kinds of official positions and he refused. When he could no longer keep the request at bay, he did not, as many did at the time, merely hold the position without working. The phrase used in Chinese for this attitude is to sit like a dead corpse in a post, eating vegetarian, i.e. not coming to grips with something and working hard like a good meat-eater. Wang Xizhi is known to have expressed frank and astute views on political situations to the Prime Minister of the time, and he is known to have opened granaries to starving people during times of famine. From a young age, he had a robust and open nature, never allowing himself to be troubled by trifling matters and he maintained this quality of "beneficence and uprightness" as an adult. This may be what makes his calligraphy so flowing and expansive, so endowed with vigor, so carefree and gladsome.

Wang Xizhi is known to have loved calligraphy from an early age. He used the calligraphed works of the

Preface for the Orchid Pavilion Poems by Wang Xizhi.

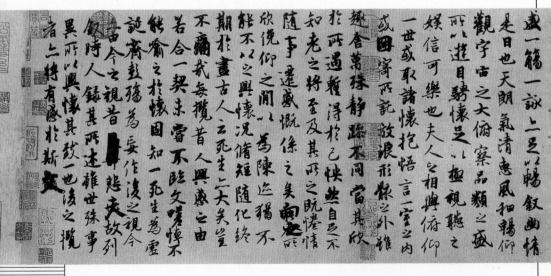

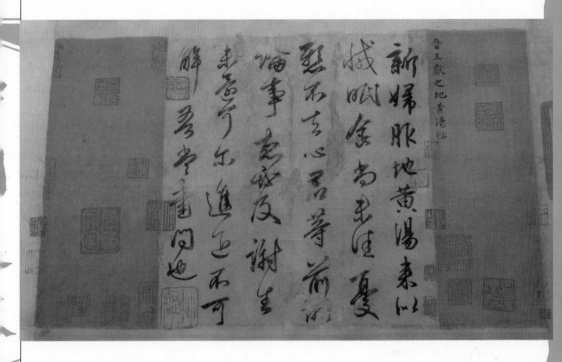

Glutinous Rehmannia Soup by Wang Xianzhi.

famous calligrapher Lady Wei as his model, also earlier great masters of calligraphy like Li Si, Cao Xi, Zhang Zhi, Zhang Chang, Cai Yong, Zhong You and Liang Hu. He combined the best attributes of their various styles and developed his own. His attainments in the various traditional shape strokes, including cursive, square, and so on, including exaggerated forms of these traditional shapes, allowed him to deepen and develop the artform.

Specific works of Wang Xizhi have been carved into models and made into rubbings, which are used as reference by calligraphers to this day. Certain works in the style of "kai-shu," or square script, are famous and much emulated. One, called *Piece Written in a Sunny Day after a Pleasant Snowfall* has only 24 characters and was included by the Qing-dynasty Emperor Qianlong in his collection of "Three Delights" for emulating as models of calligraphic script. The *Preface for the Orchid Pavilion Poems* is his most famous work. It is admired from a literary perspective as much as for its calligraphy, for its expansive and feeling nature. From a calligraphic

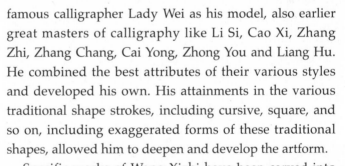

perspective, it has been crowned with high acclaim by generations of calligraphers as worthy of respectful study. Wang Xizhi's son succeeded him as a calligrapher (Wang Xianzhi, 344–386), and became a fine artist in his own right, contributing to further development of the art. His *Mid-Autumn Scroll* is written in cursive script, and is only 22 characters long, but is a unique masterpiece. Emperor Qianlong similarly put this work among his "Three Delights," regarding it as a national treasure. The son and the father are equally famous and therefore known as the Two Wangs.

The Yungang Grottoes and the Spread of Buddhism in China

The Yungang Grottoes are situated on the northern banks of the Wuzhou River, at the foot of Wuzhou mountain range around sixteen kilometers to the west of Datong City in Shanxi Province. The stone grottoes are carved into the hillside and extend for one kilometer in an east-west direction. Forty-five primary grottoes remain today, but there are a total of some 1,100 smaller ones containing altogether some 51,000 carved statues. This is one of the largest groupings of stone grottoes in China, famed throughout the world as an

The main budha in No.20 grotto, a sitting statue of Sakyamuni, with a height of 13.7 meters.

Bodhisattva statue at the west side of the north wall in the atria of No.9 grotto.

artistic treasury; the grottoes are among the first protected national monuments of China.

Carving of the grottoes and their statues began in 460 and proceeded for some sixty years, during the Northern Wei period and over the course of the reigns of several dynastic rulers. Carving began after a period which is described in history as "Taiwu annihilates Buddhism," favorably helped by a period described as "Wencheng restores the law." Emperor Wencheng's "peaceful" reign years (460–465) began the largescale carving of the Yungang Grottoes, and they were basically completed by the fifth year of the Zhengguang reign of Emperor Xiaoming (524). The senior monk is said to have begun

budha with his feet crossed in No.13 grotto, small statues of budha serve as the supporting point of the grand statue of budha, pretty and stable.

the work, with five grottoes that are now described as Grottoes 16 to 20. Most of the existing grottoes were carved before the 18th year of the Taihe reign (494), when the capital was moved to Luoyang. The artistry of the Yungang Grottoes is considered to be the grandest and most magnificent among the three main Buddhist grottoes in China, the others being at Mogao and Dunhuang. The smallest Buddhist sculpture is a mere 2 centimeters high, the largest is 17 meters high. Most depict various aspects of religious deities. There are also many reproductions in stone of wooden architecture, finely wrought details of ornamentation and design, musical instruments, and outstanding relief works of Buddhist paraphernalia. The carving style continues and builds on the sculptural traditions of Qin and Han, but has also absorbed and blended in the refinements of Buddhist arts, so that it has its own unique artistic style. The stone grottoes at Yungang deeply influenced the later development of Sui

Bodhi tree and two budhas sitting face to face.

Dancer and musician at the top of No.12 grotto.

and Tang arts, and are a testament to cultural exchange and the interaction of China with other Asian countries.

Buddhism originated in India, begun by Sakyamuni. After the Buddha reached Nirvana, his disciples continued to transmit Buddhist doctrines and the teachings came into China in the first century BC. The Han Emperor Mingdi (reigned 58–75 AD), invited Buddhists from the "western regions" to live at the White Horse Temple in Luoyang, where they began to translate the "Forty-Two sutras." This was China's first Buddhist canon. The Eastern-Han scholar Muzi (c.170 –?) swept away obstacles to the spread of Buddhism in China with his interpretation of the "spirit" of Taoism, Confucianism, and Buddhism being the same. The Indian monk Kumarajive (343–413) came to China after this and undertook the translation of a number of Buddhist works including the *Diamond Sutra* and the *Lotus Sutra* among others. Four large centers of translation were established at China's largest cities at the time: Yecheng, Chang'an, Nanjing, and Wuwei. Buddhist doctrines achieved notable progress in the northern region of the

Famen Temple of Fufeng, Shaanxi

Northern and Southern Dynasties where the rulers of the Later Zhao and Early Qin were avid devotees. They liaised with high monks both inside and outside China, had sutras translated, built monasteries and temples, burned incense and prayed to the Buddha. The spread of Buddhism was not without setbacks, however. Emperor Taiwudi of Northern Wei (reigned 423–452) repressed the teachings, had believers killed, destroyed temples and inflicted considerable damage on anything Buddhist. His grandson, Xiaowendi (reigned 471–499) began to change this completely when he assumed the throne by reinstating oppressed believers. It was this emperor who decided that stone grottoes should be created outside the capital city of Pingcheng, which is the modern-day Datong. The carving of stone statues of Buddhism was considered a part of his atonement. The result was the famous Yungang Grottoes.

Buddhism was supported by a number of other devout believers among emperors after this, and other grottoes were begun, notably the stone grottoes at Longmen in Henan. In addition to the Mogao grottoes at Dunhuang, which had begun earlier, China's largest treasury of stone artwork was completed. The Southern Emperor Liang Wudi (reigned 502–549) was an ardent believer, almost to the extent of disregarding all else. He undertook great building of Buddhist temples. The Tang-dynasty poet Du Mu wrote a poem that commemorates the building at the time, noting the 480 temples of the Southern dynasties untold numbers of towers in the rain and mists. In fact, this number greatly underestimates the total. There were more than 2,000 temples in Nanjing alone. Liang Wudi left home four times to travel as an itinerant monk, and paid so little attention to matters of court that the government was overturned. Henan King Hou Jing took advantage of the chaotic situation to lock Liang Wudi up in a tower where he simply starved to death.

The Buddhist master Bodhidharma came to China shortly after this. It was no longer possible to gain support from the emperor, so he traveled to Mt. Songshan where he sat facing a wall in profound meditation for nine years. He became known as the First Patriarch of Chan or Zen Buddhism. His robe and alms bowl were passed on to the Second Patriarch Huike, the Third Sengcan, the Fourth Daoxin, the Fifth Hongren, and the Sixth, the famous Huineng. Through their efforts, Buddhism in China advanced to a new stage. In the Tang Dynsty, Buddhism enjoyed a revival due to the work of two monks who brought sutras from India to the capital of Chang'an, where they translated them. These were the famous Faxian and Xuanzang, later immortalized in the literary work known in English as *Travels to the West*. The plot of that work follows the travels of Xuanzang to India, but the real Xuanzang did not have as his stalwart companions the characters of Sun Wukong (the monkey) and Zhu Bajie (the pig). After a period of intense struggles between those who opposed Buddhism and those who

White Horse Temple in Luoyang, Henan

supported it, acceptance of the doctrine finally gained the upper hand. The Tang Emperor Gaozong (reigned 649–683) secreted sacred remains of the Buddha in a reliquary under a temple in Shaanxi. In the 1980s, this repository of treasures under Famensi or Famen Temple in Fufeng was officially excavated and brought to light 1,300 years later.

Religion was generally not held in high regard in China. Taoism exerted a certain influence; Confucianism was not regarded as a religion. Buddhism did come to receive strong official support, however, and was in fact more widespread in China than in its country of origin. Buddhism has several distinguishing characteristics in China: first, in the process of transmission, it gradually adapted to China's longstanding culture. Second, it was accompanied by the widespread translation of Buddhist sutras, building of temples, and carving of stone grottoes, all of which left a strong cultural legacy in China. Today, the most famous of China's tourist sights are associated with Buddhist temples or stone grottoes. Protecting this religious cultural legacy is a common responsibility of all Chinese. China already has a number of sites that are listed as World Heritage Sites by UNESCO: The Mogao Grottoes of Dunhuang, the Potala of Lhasa, the Grottoes of Yungang, the Grottoes of Longmen, the Carvings of Dazu, and so on. These provide an arena for the appreciation of Buddhist arts by friends from all over the world.

The Grand Canal and the End of the Sui Dynasty

The famous canal that connects Beijing and Hangzhou is the longest manmade canal in the world. It extends for 1,794 kilometers and has been important in linking both the economies and the cultures of north and south China. It passes through the six provinces and municipalities: Beijing, Hebei, Tianjin, Shandong, Jiangsu, and Zhejiang, and it connects five great water systems: the Yellow River, the Huai River, the Yangtze River, the Qiantang River, and the canal itself.

Construction of the Jing-Hang Canal, as it is known in Chinese, began in the year 486 BC. Waters were finally linked up from one end to the other in 1293, meaning that the work extended over a period of 1,779 years. In

Yangzhou, Han'gou site of the Grand Canal from Beijing to Hangzhou.

Map of the canal in the Sui Dynasty.

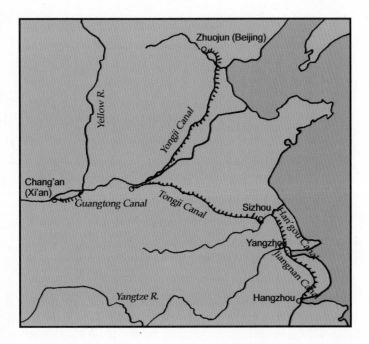

the course of these years, the canal went through three major stages of construction and renovation.

The first was during the 5th century BC, in the latter part of the Spring and Autumn Period. At the time, the ruler of the state of Wu, south of the Yangtze River, was attempting to usurp the position of the warlord of the Central Plains. He needed a logistical supply route for his armies. He mobilized labor to construct the canal from what is now Yangzhou towards the northeast, passing through Sheyang Lake to Huai-an, and entering the Huai River. Water from the Yangtze River was led into the Huai River, and this stretch of 170 kilometers became the earliest section of the Canal.

The second stage was in the early 7th century when the Sui Dynasty (581–618) reunified the country. This became the primary period of canal construction. The second Emperor of the Sui decided to move the capital to Luoyang in order to enable control of the vast area south of the Yangtze River. To allow the rich products of the Yangtze River delta area to be transported to Luoyang, he ordered the extension of the previous canal. It is said

that he also wanted to create an aesthetic enjoyment for people of the rich and populous area around Yangzhou as they boated from Luoyang down to Yangzhou. In the year 605, he mandated the cutting of a canal of over 1,000 kilometers extending from Luoyang to Qingjiang in Jiangsu Province, a place now known as Huaiyin. Water was diverted from the Yellow River, curved its way toward the southeast, then merged the waters of the Luo River, the Yellow River and the Huai. This was known as the Tongji Canal. In 608, he ordered that the canal be extended by another 1,000 kilometers towards the north, to a place to the southwest of current Beijing. This section was then known as the Yongji Canal. In 610, he again ordered that a 400 kilometers' section be cut from Zhenjiang in Jiangsu province to Hangzhou in Zhejiang province. This section was then called the Jiangnan Canal ("south of the river" canal). At the time, Hangzhou was the major port city doing foreign trade in China. Han' gou Canal was also reconstructed. A canal that extended 1,700 kilometers and linked Hangzhou and Luoyang was then ready, which could allow the passage of boats transporting goods.

The Sui Dynasty had reunified China after the long period of fragmented rule known as the Three Kingdoms, Two Jins, and Northern and Southern Dynasties. Reunification provided opportunities for economic and social development and the early Sui period did indeed see tremendous advances. The book *One Hundred People who have changed the Fate of Mankind* includes Sui Emperor Wendi (name: Yang Jian) as one of the world's great men of history. Yang Jian's successor, Sui Yangdi (name: Yang Guang), quickly reversed this situation however with annual military campaigns and a despotic rule that disregarded the people's welfare. He not only lost territory, he also lost his head. Nonetheless, the canal that he contributed to repairing and maintaining left a rich legacy for later generations. It was important in the unification of the country, in economic development, in the growth of cities along the way, in ease of transporting goods and in enriching cultural intercourse. As a result,

the Grand Canal became a vital artery in China between north and south.

In Jiangsu Province, transportation on the canal is still busy.

The third stage in building the canal came after the Mongol-ruled Yuan Dynasty (1271–1368) established their capital in Beijing in the 13th century. In order to link north and south directly without having to go around by way of Luoyang, the Yuan Dynasty invested ten years in digging out sections between the Luozhou River and the Huitong River. This then linked up the natural river and lake system between Tianjin and Jiangsu's Qingjiang. To the south of Qingjiang the canal linked up with the previous constructions all the way to Hangzhou. The original section of canal between Beijing and Tianjin had been abandoned, so a new "Tonghui Canal" was rebuilt. After this, the new Jing-Hang Canal was shorter than the original by more than 900 kilometers.

In 2006, China began the application for World Heritage for the Jing-Hang Canal. In announcing this

Wu Bridge West Road
Dock in Wuxi, still with
many sails.

project, the government pointed out, "The Jing-Hang
Canal is a manifestation of our country's superiority
over the world in water engineering and transport and
it has been bequeathed to us as a rich legacy. It nurtured
the development of many famous cities, it provided a
foundation for cultural richness, it precipitated all kinds
of information exchange regarding our country's political,
economic, cultural, and social conditions. The Grand
Canal, together with the Great Wall, are the symbol of
the high status of Chinese culture itself. Protecting the
canal has tremendous significance in the transmission of
humankind's civilization and the harmonious integration
of society."

Although endowed with tremendous capabilities,
Sui Emperor Yangdi (569–618) was eventually unable to
restrain his own crazy desires, and he paid a high price
for his rapacious rule. The second son of Sui Wendi, he
had seized the throne in 604 and then governed as one

of China's most ruthless rulers. In deciding to move the capital to Luoyang, he conscripted a labor force of two million men to build the city. To the west of Luoyang he built the Western Garden—a striking site with its towers and pavilions set in an area of more than 200 mu. He used the garden for leisure and entertainment, viewing sights with several thousand palace women on horseback, enjoying banquets, leading a dissolute life. In the process of constructing the Grand Canal, he is said to have used 150 million workers, many of whom perished of exhaustion. When he found one stretch to be too shallow, in a fury he ordered that 50,000 officials and workers be buried alive. From August 605, he passed through the canal to Jiangdu three times on inspection tours. He rode in a great dragon boat, 200 feet long, 45 wide, and four stories high. Concubines, officials, eunuchs and monks accompanied him on several thousand other boats: the entourage is said to have extended some 200 *li*. 80,000 men were employed just in hauling the boats along. Protective armies on horseback patrolled the banks of the canal on

Randeng Pagoda in Tongzhou, Beijing, built in the last years of Northern Zhou, before the excavation of the Sui canal. It stands at the north bank of the canal and witnessed more than 1,300 years of water transportation on the canal.

either side. The populace in the vicinity were forced to contribute food and drink for this traveling city. Yang Guang initiated war three times against Korea. The carpenters building boats worked day and night to make ready, and it is said that three or four out of every ten died. The navy of the Sui and the army attacked Korea on two fronts, each of the three attempts was repulsed and ended in defeat. The rich reserves that had been built up during the period of Sui Wendi were exhausted. The fields began to go bare, a scorched landscape covered the land, farmers had nothing to eat but bark and leaves. In 611, a peasants revolt erupted. Yang Guang continued, however, to lead his dissolute life. In 618, the Right-flank General Yuwen Huaji stole into the palace and strangled the Emperor, after which the Sui Dynasty was destroyed. In total, it had existed for 38 years and been ruled by two men.

Chang'an and Tri-colored Glazed Pottery: the Flourishing Tang

The city of Xi'an, which in ancient times was also known as Chang'an and Jing Zhao, is today the capital city of Shaanxi Province. It is one of China's most famous historic and cultural sites. Located on the southern banks of the Wei River in the Guanzhong Plain, it enjoys the benefit of rich earth created by several large river systems.

As a result, Xi'an has been one of China's seven ancient capitals. The others are Luoyang, Nanjing, Beijing, Kaifeng, Hangzhou, and Anyang. Among these, it is the most ancient and, with 3,000 years of history, the one with the longest past. It has seen the passage of many dynasties, from early Western Zhou (1134 BC) all the way up to Tang (618–907). Western Zhou, Qin, Western Han, Xin, Western Jin, Early Zhao, Early Qin, Later Qin, Western Wei, Northern Zhou, Sui, and Tang all had their

Portrait of Tang Emperor Taizong

capitals here. Among the seven early capitals of China, Xi'an had the most extensive building. Chang'an's streets and alleys and markets, and the palaces of Han and Tang dynasties give one an unforgettable sense of magnificent grandeur. Today, the famous historic sites dotted around Xi'an include: Banpo Museum, Great Goose Pagoda, Stelae Woods, Huaqing Pond, Qin Tomb and the Terracotta Warriors, Mao Ling (imperial tomb), Qian Ling (imperial tomb), Famen Temple, and others.

In 1982, Xi'an became one of the first registered historic cultural cities in China.

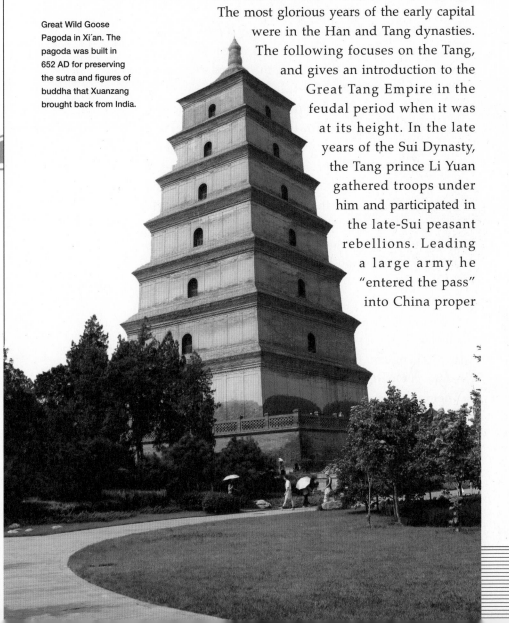

Great Wild Goose Pagoda in Xi'an. The pagoda was built in 652 AD for preserving the sutra and figures of buddha that Xuanzang brought back from India.

The most glorious years of the early capital were in the Han and Tang dynasties. The following focuses on the Tang, and gives an introduction to the Great Tang Empire in the feudal period when it was at its height. In the late years of the Sui Dynasty, the Tang prince Li Yuan gathered troops under him and participated in the late-Sui peasant rebellions. Leading a large army he "entered the pass" into China proper

and in 618 declared the establishment of a new dynasty. Its reign name was called Wude and its capital was at Chang'an (Xi'an). This then began the period of Chinese history when the Li family ruled China as the Tang Dynasty. In the 9th year of Wude (626), the second son of Li Yuan, Li Shimin, with the assistance of certain important ministers, mobilized the "Xuanwumen Coup." He put to death those opposing him, his elder brother Li Jiancheng and his youger brother Li Yuanji, and he forced his father Li Yuan off the throne. Ruling now as Emperor, he changed the reign name to Zhenguan, and he began his long rule as the famous Tang Taizong. Tang Taizong, or Li Shimin, was a most capable emperor among rulers in Chinese history. Although the path of his assuming power may not have been the most enlightened and virtuous, nevertheless his rule in both military and civil matters was one of splendid achievements. In the second year of Zhenguan, Emperor Taizong ordered his army's general, Li Duan, to declare war on the Tujue (Turks). Li Duan was greatly successful, obliterating the threat of various western tribes against the Central Plains. He then began to "open up" the northwest. At the same time, Emperor Taizong used highly capable ministers as his most important assistants, and they organized governmental affairs in a stable and secure fashion. He passed a series of legal, economic, and cultural reforms, leading the Great Tang Empire to previously unknown

Bunian Painting by Yan Liben. The painting is on the theme of the historic event of the marriage between Tibetan chief Songtsen Gampo and Tang Princess Wencheng.

Tri-colored glazed
pottery of a band on
camel: a mini band sits
on the back of a camel,
with a girl dancing in the
middle. Kept in Shaanxi
History Museum.

heights. The Zhenguan period is justly renowned in Chinese history.

In the fourth month of the twenty-third year of Zhenguan (649), Tang Taizong was overturned by his ninth son, who assumed the throne with a new reign name of Yongwei. The ninth son then became Tang Gaozong. After assuming the throne, Gaozong continued to implement the policies of Taizong so that his reign continued the legacy of the Zhenguan reign. In 655, the sixth year of his reign, Tang Gaozong set up Wu Zetian as empress and Wu Zetian began to oversee governmental affairs. In 683, Gaozong died of illness. In the ninth month of 690, the sixty-seven-year-old Wu Zetian changed the reign name of the dynasty to Zhou and began to rule as emperor herself, in her own name. She became the only female emperor to formally be declared as and rule as empress in China. Although she had usurped power, and was later denounced for consolidating power in her own hands, nonetheless the political and economic situation of the Tang Dynasty continued to move forward during her reign. She had a book published on agricultural practices and greatly developed agricultural production. She created the conditions for a substantial improvement in the material wealth of Tang-dynasty lives. However, during the latter part of her reign she doted on one minister and became very dissatisfied with her premier. In 705, the Premier Zhang Jianzhi and others mobilized a palace coup that forced her off the throne. The previous Tang-dynasty reign name was restored. In a final struggle for imperial power, Li Longji defeated the Empress Wei group and assumed the throne. He changed his reign name to Kaiyuan, and became Tang Xuanzong (reigned 712–756). Xuanzong was a very enlightened ruler, as successor to Li Shimin. He made adjustments in political power, reformed the administrative and military systems, encouraged economic development, reformed the tax system, he revised the waterworks, and generally brought the people to a status they had never before enjoyed. The poet Du Fu has written admiringly of the "flourishing time of Kaiyuan."

From the time the Tang Dynasty was established up to the years of Kaiyuan, a number of enlightened rulers, including Li Shimin and Wu Zetian, administered the country. In terms of foreign relations, the Tang Dynasty continued the practice of the Sui and gradually run its administration by three ministries called Zhongshu, Menxia, and Shangshu, all of which strengthened the power of the emperor's rule. At the same time, Tang reformed the exam system of the Sui dynasty, making it into an important method and shortcut to finding excellent officials. In addition, to strengthen relations with miniority peoples on the border, Li Shimin adopted a "hard and soft" approach. In 641, or the 15th year of Zhenguan, he married Princess Wencheng to Songtsen Gampo, which pulled Tibet into a tighter liaison with the Great Tang. The renowned "Silk Road" also became an

Tri-color glazed pottery of a sitting girl figure.

important conduit at the time for the Central Plains to develop towards the outside, to improve relations with foreigners, to increase economic and cultural exchange.

With few internal or external worries, Tang Dynasty was able to expand and advance in an unprecedented way. The humanities and arts of the early Tang period developed briskly. Poetry, calligraphy, and painting saw the appearance of a number of famous artists. Those poets included "the four outstandings of early Tang," Wang Wei (699–759), Cen Shen (715–770), and the two greatest poets Li Bai (701–762) and Du Fu (712–770). In addition to these were the great masters of painting, Wu Daozi and Li Sixun, the calligraphers Yan Zhenqing and Liu Gongquan, and the musician Li Guinian. All were representative of Tang-dynasty cultural talent.

Tang *sancai* (tri-colored glazed pottery) is one of the marvels of handicrafts of the Tang era, which competes in technical excellence with our arts today.

Tang sancai is the term applied to a kind of ceramic that is glazed with different colors and that was used in both daily life and as an article in funerary practices to accompany the deceased. The colors include green, blue, yellow, white, red, and orange, but the primary colors are yellow, green and orange, so it is called sancai or tri-colored. Many types of objects were made with this form of ceramic, including human and animal figurines and various shapes of pots. The primary production places of sancai were Luoyang and Chang'an, also some parts of Henan and Shaanxi. In the process of making the ceramic, the glaze was allowed to run down naturally, so that the results were often strange and wonderful and no two were ever exactly the same. The artistic creation of Tang sancai reflected the special nature of the age and of society at the time. The warrior figures are fierce and robust, the horses are magnificent steeds, and the camels are vigorous. All are well endowed with the vigor and strength of early Tang. From the plumpness of the faces of ladies, one can see also that this was a period when plumpness was considered a mark of beauty.

Along the River during Pure Brightness Day: Kaifeng, a Flourishing Northern Song City

A long handscroll resides among the treasures of the Beijing Palace Museum. Painted by the Song-dynasty painter Zhang Zeduan, it is known as *Along the River during Pure Brightness Day*. It depicts the scenery, architecture, and people along the way and is a masterpiece, an absolute treasure. It is one of the most famous paintings in the history of Chinese painting. In

Part of *Along the River during Pure Brightness Day.*

Part of *Along the River during Pure Brightness Day.*

addition to its artistic quality, surrounding its allure are many stories that have come down through the ages.

The painting is 24.8 cm high and roughly 528 cm long. The painter Zhang Zeduan was a Shandong man from Wucheng. In his youth, he went to the capital city then known as Bian to study. During the reign of Emperor Huizong he was appointed to Hanlin Academy and applied himself exclusively to painting.

The exquisite brushwork of the painting records the capital city of Bian at the latter period of the Northern Song Dynasty (960–1127), during the reign of Huizong. It depicts the city and river, with inhabitants, architecture, along the precincts just outside the city. The work is in the form of a long scroll, meant to be viewed sequentially as it is unrolled, so that the complex scene of the painting is both unified and full of changes. The attire and expressions of the people depicted are all different, and they are engaged in all kinds of activities. The dynamic quality of their movement is vigorous, the composition

Part of *Along the River during Pure Brightness Day.*

is detailed and has a rhythm of harmonious changes, the brushwork is marvelous. The scroll is divided into three stages or sections.

Part of *Along the River during Pure Brightness Day.*

The first section is in the mist, with sparse trees and partially obscured thatch huts, bridges, running water, old trees, and boats. Two footmen are herding donkeys with packs loaded with coal. The top of a bridge is decorated with willows and various flowers, there are men riding horses, men shouldering carrying poles, they are all returning from the outskirts of the city where they have been sweeping graves. This section sets the time as Pure Brightness Day and establishes the setting as a kind of prelude to the rest of the painting. The middle section shows scenes along the banks of the Bian River, with grain transport boats tethered to the shore, with the awnings of many shops. Passersby are engaged in a variety of activities, resting in teahouses, getting their fortunes told, eating at shops. All is bustling and lively. In the river, boats are either being hauled by pullers or rocked by men with poles, all piled high with goods, many are docked at the banks getting their products unloaded. Crossing over the span of the river is a large bridge of wooden construction, something like a flying rainbow. One large boat is just waiting to pass through the opening of its arch, with people both inside and outside the boat busily preparing. The last section features a large city tower. There are teashops, wineshops, shops for footwear, butchers, and temples. In the shops are all manner of goods and customers, precious incense and paper horses for burning at the graves, there are apothecaries on both sides, cart repair, fortune telling, all kinds of trades and all kinds of people, from peddlers to gentlemen to scholars to the townspeople. Barefooted monks, visitors from the countryside, children listening to stories, sons of wealthy families drinking to their fill, men, women, old and young, scholars, farmers, workers, tradesmen, people of all religions and persuasions pass

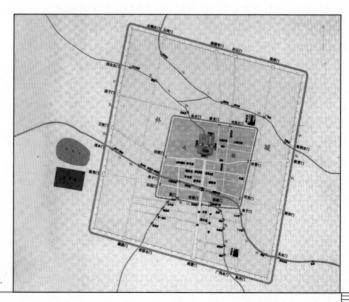

Map of the East Capital of Northern Song. The East Capital is also called the capital of Bian.

along. The humanity in the painting is itself flowing like a river that never stops.

In the total length of approximately five meters of painting, the painting depicts over 550 types of people, also some fifty or sixty animals, plus twenty bridges and more than twenty boats. The bridges and city towers are careful in detail, showing the special construction of Song-Dynasty architecture.

This Northern-Song-Dynasty painting shows one corner of life in the capital of Bian. It shows a high level of economic attainment, of agriculture, handicrafts, a flourishing commerce, a culture that is fast developing and that put emphasis on intellectuals. In military matters, however, the Northern Song was extremely weak. In order to strengthen its military defenses it expended a large amount on its army, to the extent that national granaries were emptied and national strength declined. Facing annual crises, the country's territory was encroached upon, soldiers had no fighting spirit and were generally defeated. The Song Emperor Huizong and his son Qinzong were taken as prisoners by the Jin army, and territories to the north of the Yellow River fell under the control of northern enemies.

Although in a defensive posture for a long time in its wars with outsiders, the Northern Song court was still able to create a glorious cultural arena inside the country. A necessary precondition for culture to flourish is a political environment that is relatively open and enlightened. It may be said that Northern Song is the only dynasty in ancient Chinese history that had a court that did not kill intellectuals just because they held different political views. It is probably due to this enlightened position that Northern Song could reach such peaks of cultural attainment in the Chinese feudal system. Because of this, Bian or Kaifeng also became the only capital city not to experience a violent transition in imperial power. Although it was not grand and mighty, still it did not labor under a shadow of shame for murdering rationality and perpetrating violence against all good conscience. On

Kaibao Temple Pagoda in Kaifeng, built in 1049 AD. During more than 900 years, it went through war, flood, earth quake, and other disasters, and still stands. Its exterior is covered with brown glaze bricks, looking like iron from afar. Since it is very firm and solid like iron, people started to call it "iron pagoda" since the Yuan Dynasty.

the contrary, looking at the glorious accomplishments that remain as evidence in the fields of literature, arts, science and technology, among many ancient cities, it uniquely possesses a propitious quality and therefore shines in the annals of history.

Grand Xiangguo Temple in Kaifeng, a famous Buddhist temple in China, built in 555 AD. In the Northern Song Dynasty, Xiangguo Temple received homage from the emperor and was expanded several times. Later it became the biggest temple in the capital and the buddhist activity center of the country.

The relatively benign governing environment of the Northern Song was built on the foundation of an approach first encouraged by the founding emperor of the dynasty, Zhao Kuangyin (960–976). A political posture of rule by the "wen" or civic side as opposed to "wu" or the military side, then became the ongoing tradition of the dynasty. Zhao Kuangyin had a painful understanding of the results of military rule dating from the closing years of the Tang Dynasty. He yearned to have "civic" officials hold the reigns to government. He aimed for a government by "good" men. In order to cultivate and protect a contingent of civic officials who were of high quality and stable in their occupations, he instituted a number of policies that are worth enumerating. One was emphasis on using old intellectuals, rediscovering their latent potential and putting it to use for the new government. These so-called "old intellectuals," simply meant those scholars who had exited from public life due to the historical background of the Five Dynasties (907–960). Generally these men had previously been officials. Zhao Kuangyin was put on the throne by a military group, but he preferred that the country be entrusted to civic officials. He carefully selected intellectuals to serve, he revised official ranks, he upgraded official quality. One outstanding aspect in this regard was his further development of the keju examination system. His careful monitoring of the examination turned it into a large-scale employment system, and overcame the influence of the practice from Han and Tang times of using warlords as the source of high officialdom. This increased the chances of advancement for small and medium-sized landowners and for the lower ranks of intellectuals. An excellent exam system gradually formed into a tradition. The later Song Dynasty produced many superlative officials who had come from impoversished families—the reason to a large degree was this healthy examination system. Extending relatively free latitude to intellectuals and ruling in a permissive political environment were conscious decisions on the part of the Emperor. A Song-dynasty writer has dcescribed the way Zhao Kuangyin erected a large stele in the sleeping chamber of the Royal Ancestral Temple. It was seven or eight feet high, and was called the Oath Stelae. The most important lines made it clear that rulers and those in power were forbidden to kill officials who presented contrary points of view, or officials who made unpleasant reports to the emperor. The wording of the Oath Stelae was simple but defined a bottom line of safety for intellectuals which was of extreme importance in motivating their intelligence, wisdom, and candid views. That so very many outstanding political, philosophical, and literary leaders emerged in the Song Dynasty was in large part due to this: the government was stable and effective and people who stood to benefit in different ways maintained balance and stability in the midst of competing with one another so that they did

Kaifeng today: the street of Song city.

not end up drawing blood. The government derived its strength from this principle of "not killing people." In the long course of Chinese history, this intelligent policy of protecting intellectuals was unique.

The development of culture and the development of commerce are closely related. Kaifeng was a prime example. Compared to management of capitals in previous dynasties, Kaifeng was a supremely commercialized city. Kaifeng destroyed the distinction that had been followed in the Chang'an capital of Sui and Tang of keeping the "lanes," or the residential section, separate from the "market," or the commercial section. It also got rid of the distinction between day and night —there were shops and wine houses everywhere, and many were open for business 24 hours a day. Night business was an important mark of a commercialized city. This was not restricted to eating and drinking; entertainment naturally was a part of the scene too. In this regard, Kaifeng could be considered a city that

benefited from break-through developments. One was the uncoupling of the entertainment business from imperial monopoly control. Only in the time of the Song dynasty did the theatrical industry finally move towards "min-jian" status, or "of the people." The theater enjoyed unprecedented development as a result. There was an infinite variety of forms of theatrical entertainment, shadow-puppets, acrobatics, singing, acting, cross-talk... Each developed its highly skilled "stars" who were adored by the public.

As an ancient city, there is no substitute for the position of Kaifeng in Chinese history. If you were to view the long course of Chinese history as a long scroll, you would see bloody scenes throughout the early and the late sections. But in the middle, in the Northern Song capital of Kaifeng, although it lasted over 160 years there was no occasion on which the people were subjected to large-scale slaughter. Intellectuals were given particular protection. Since they were living under an autocratic rule, this was all the more a matter to be celebrated. Why is this painting by Zhang Zeduan so treasured by people throughout the ages? One important reason may be because viewers see an ideal lifestyle in the painting. They catch glimpses of bygone times and recognize hopes that are worthy of preserving.

The Grave of Yue Fei and the War against Jin

The grave of Yue Fei is located at the north bank of the west section of Beishan Road, at the northwest corner of West Lake by the south side of Qixia Hill in Hangzhou, Zhejiang. It's the place to commemorate the national hero, Yue Fei. Yue Fei (1103–1142) grew up in Tangyin County of Henan and became a major figure in Southern Song (1127–1279) as a general in the war against Jin. Yue Fei came from a peasant family. He is extremely obedient and followed the slogan that his mother punctured on his back, "loyal to the country." He had been abiding by this rule all his life. He joined the army in 1126 and

Painting about Yue Fei's mother tattooing on his back.

The statue of Yue Fei in the Yue Temple of Hangzhou.

repeatly gained battle achievements. He was promoted from a soldier to a marshal. He established the Yue Troop, which was very disciplined and brave. Their spirit made the Jin (1115–1234) soldiers moaned, "It's easier to shake a mountain than to shake the Yue Troop!" Yue Fei commanded 126 battles in his life and never once was defeated. He once led his troop and reoccupied the fallen capital Jiankang (Nanjing). He had led his troop north and reoccupied Luoyang and Shangzhou. But each vistory was destroyed by the court of Southern Song that preferred to enjoy peace and feared war.

In 1140, General Wuzhu of Jin led four troops to conquer the South. The Yue Troop fought vigorously and achieved victory in Yancheng. They occupied Zhuxian Town and were just 45 kilometers from Kaifeng. They claimed to destroy the head quarter of the enemy and celebrate afterwards. However, the Song Emperor Zhao Gou and Prime Minister Qin Hui wanted to sue for peace and commanded Yue Fei to return after the vistory. Yue Fei returned with tears in his eyes and deeply sighed,

Folk art of Yue Fei's life.

"Ten years of effort is down the drains in one day. All the acquired states are finished in one day. It is hard for our country to prosper again. We have lost the world!" Yue Fei was immediately dismissed from his post. Zhao Gou and Qin Hui then instigated Zhang Jun and Moqi Xie to make false testimony and frame a case against Yue Fei. Yue Fei was put to prison for the accusal of rebellion. Yue Fei griefly wrote "The sun can clear the evidence! The sun can clear the evidence!" to express his emotions. Wuzhu then passed the information, "Song must kill Yue Fei and they will agree to peace." Zhou Gou and Qin Hui complied to the enemy's indication and decided to kill Yue Fei. In 1142, Yue Fei, his son Yue Yun, and his subordinate Zhang Xian were killed at Fengbo Kiosk. Yue Fei was at the age of 39. Another general Han Shizhong interrogated Qin Hui what crime Yue Fei had committed. Qin Hui answered reluctantly, "Might be." Han Shizhong solemnly said, "How can 'might be' persuade the country?" After Yue Fei was killed, some loyal people moved the corpses out and buried them at the bank of West Lake. After 21 years, the unjust charge of Yue Fei was reversed during the Xiaozong reign and Yue Fei was homaged as Lord E. The glorious battle achievements and the tragic end of Yue Fei aroused admiration and

sympathy of the Chinese people through time. He was regarded as number one hero in Chinese history. The poetry he wrote during his northern expedition is very well known through the following centuries till today:

The Whole River Red

Rage bristling under the cap,
I lean against the railing;
The rushing rain has ceased.
Lifting my eyes,
Towards the sky I let out a battle cry;
My blood is boiling.
Thirty years: rank and honour, just so much dust;
Eight hundred leagues: travelling with the moon
  and clouds.
Do not let it slip away;
When a young man's head turns grey,
Regret will be too late.

The national insult
Is yet to be avenged;
Your servants' shame:
When will it be erased?
Let us ride the long chariots
To crush those mountain strongholds.

Four generals during the resurgence in Southern Song.

The Grave of Yue Fei.

Kneeling statues of Qin Hui and his wife in the
Yue Temple of Hangzhou.

Yue Fei's homeland: the
Yue Temple in Tangyin,
Henan.

Glorious quest: to feast on the flesh of the invaders.
We laugh and chat and quench our thirst with
Tartar blood.
Let us start
To take back our rivers and mountains,
And report to the Heavenly Palace.

The grave of Yue Fei lies in the Temple of Yue Fei today
and it has become a tourist site. The Temple of Yue Fei
was constructed from 1221 of the Southern Song Dynasty.
Today's temple had been reconstructed twice in the Qing
Dynasty (1644–1911) and during the Republic of China
(1912–1949). The temple appears majestic. Inside the hall
stands the polychrome statue of Yue Fei. A huge plaque is
hung above with Yue Fei's grass style calligraphy, "Return
my country." At the right hand side of the hall is the grave
of Yue Fei, surrounded by blocks. On the gravestone is
the characters that says "the grave of Lord E Yue Fei." His
son Yue Yun's grave is right beside his grave. On the sides
of the grave path are terracotta warriors, stone horses,
stone tigers, and stone sheep by Ming artists. Down the

stairs of the grave path on both sides are four kneeling statues in iron fence. They are Qin Hui, Qin Hui's wife Wang, Moqi Xie, and Zhang Jun, who plot the murder of Yue Fei. They are each with their hands behind their back, kneeling before the grave and receiving everyone's spit and curse. Just as a couplet inscripted before the Yue Fei grave says, "The green mountains have the fortune to bury the loyal bones, the white iron is relentless to cast the evil minister." On a wall at the front of the grave path, Ming artist Hong Zhu had written the characters "loyal to the country." On the north and south sides are halls of steles, displaying hundreds of stone steles of different dynasties. There is another temple of Yue Fei in Yue Fei's homeland, Tangyin of Henan.

The Southern Song Dynasty is a weak regime constituted in Hangzhou by Zhao Gou after Northern Song was destroyed by Jin. Facing intimidation from the Jin, the group that claimed for peace and the group that claimed to fight had undergone long term and vigorous confrontation. The group that claimed for peace was represented by Zhao Gou and Qin Hui. And the group that claimed to fight was represented by Yue Fei, Han Shizhong, Liu Qi, and Hu Quan. Although Southern Song was weak, it possesses the rich land of southern China, plenty of fund and grains, experienced and adamant troops led by Yue Fei and Han shizhong, and the aspiration of Chinese people to reoccupy the north. If the government was united and in good faith, the war against the Jin was optimistic. They discarded the holy responsibility to defend the country and the people. They had become sinners forever. Throughout the Southern Song Dynasty, the opposition between the two parties had existed the whole time. It had become the lifeline of Southern Song and had been sung by Song poets repeatedly. When the country was in peril, Yue Fei stood out boldly and dedicated his life to the country. He held back the invasion of the Jin troops and became the national hero forever.

The *Travels of Marco Polo* and the Prosperity of the Yuan Dynasty

arco Polo left Venice for the East in the year 1271. During the war between Venice and Genoa in 1298, Marco Polo was caught and put to prison, where he dictated his travels in the East and a writer named Rustigielo in the same cell put down in writing. The notes was later titled *Travels in the East*, also named the *Travels of Marco Polo*.

Marco Polo arrived in the capital of Yuan, Dadu (Beijing), in 1275 and traveled for 17 years in China. He was appointed as government official by Kublai Khan and participated in governmental affairs. He had traveled to many parts of China including the North,

Monument of Marco Polo launching out at the shore of Quanzhou, Fujian.

Statue of Marco Polo in Lakeshore Park in Hangzhou.

the Northwest, the Southwest, and the East. In his travels, Marco Polo recorded the political and social situations, customs and religion, products and anecdotes of China and other Asian countries. His writing was direct and vividly interesting. It served as a window for the occidental to know China. Writings about China constitutes about one third of the whole work. Prosperous life in Dadu and Yangzhou was depicted in details in his recording. He portrayed the composition of the city of Beijing, the palace architecture, the festival ceremonies of the Emperor, and hunting activities. He was especially passionate towards the beautiful Hangzhou. There were 1.6 million houses in the streets of Hangzhou. The banks along the canal were elegant. There were many canals and ditches, and the water system was very convenient. There were 3,000 bathing ponds. The residents loved cold baths, but they treated the foreigners well by serving them with hot baths. Marco Polo also recorded his travels in the backland of China. The dignified quality of the

Chinese was put in action when they rather be killed than be humiliated. Many powerless people hanged themselves in front of the wealthy officials' houses for dignity purpose. After someone's death, his family will make paper figures, paper horses, and paper money according to the custom. There was a great deal of poison grass at the suburb of Suzhou, Gansu. Thousands of horses were poisoned by the grass. Sichuan people collected muskiness under the belly of muskdeer. He also recorded about beautiful concubines and the method to test if the bride was a virgin by pigeon eggs, etc.

Marco Molo was not a writer who only recorded the good side of the Yuan Dynasty. He had also honestly depicted racism in persecution in his work. He recorded the relentlessness of the Mongolians who slaughtered twenty thousand disobedient residents on the way when the corpse of Genghis Khan was escorted back home. The government official of Kublai Khan, Ahmad, clawed money from the people and tyrannized the Han people. He was later killed by revolting Han people. When Mongolians invaded the south of China, they massacred towns of people. The Han residents were extremely hostile towards the Mongolians and the Yuan regime. The residents of Changzhou placed wine jars outside of the town when the Mongolians attacked. The Mongolians were fuddled and massacred the whole town when they awoke.

Portrait of the Yuan Emperor Kublai.

In 1289, Kublai sent Marco Polo to escort Princess Kukachin to Il Khanate (now Iran) to marry a khan. Marco Polo set out with 14 giant ships in the spring of 1291. They departed from Quanzhou and arrived at Persia via Sumatra and India.

The Yuan Dynasty (1271–1368) was a regime constituted by the Mongolians. It was the first regime governing the whole China by a minority. The Mongolians is an ancient nomad people. In the 12th century, Chief Temujin was made the Khan by all the tribes and was named Genghis Khan. The Mongolians grandually became powerful. It destroyed Western Xia (1038–1227) in 1227 and destroyed Jin (1115–1234) in 1234. It was ready to unite China. After Genghis Khan died, Ogedei, Mongke, and Khublai successively held over the Khan. Their territory enlarged and they established the Mongolian empire constituted of four khanates. Their territory included today's Russia, most part of Europe, the east bank of the Mediterranean Sea, the valleys of the two rivers Tigris and Euphrates, Persia, and the northwest part of India. The four khanates were actually a combo under military conquest. They have developed into independent countries.

In 1271, Genghis Khan's grandson Khublai established the Yuan Dynasty in Dadu and was named the First

Map of the Yuan Dynasty

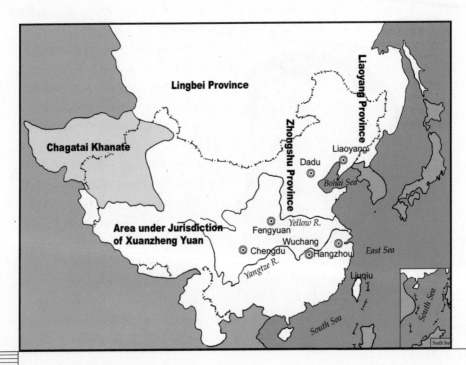

The mausoleum of Genghis Khan in Erdos, Inner Mongolia

Emperor of Yuan. From then on, Beijing has become the political, economic, and cultural center in China for the next 700 years. In 1276, the Yuan troops attacked the capital of Southern Song, Lin'an (Hangzhou) and united China. The territory of Yuan reached Mongolia and Siberia to the north, the South China Sea to the south, Tibet and Yunnan to the southwest, west Xingjiang to the northwest, and exterior Xinggan Mountains and Okhotsk Sea to the northeast. The area reached 12 million square kilometers. China's domain was laid out until the Qing Dynasty. The Mongolians joined China as a minority group since then.

After Kublai united China, he had twice conquered Japan, Annam (north Vietnam), and Burma. He had made Korea, Burma, and Annam to become dependencies of the Yuan Dynasty. Domestically, he devided people into four classes, the Mongolians, Color-eyed people (including Muslins and people in the western territory), Han in the north, and Han in the south. The status of Han people was very low. Han people became the target for Mongolians and Color-eyed people to enslave and depredate. Therefore, conflicts among the ethnic groups became a main thread of warfare, especially when the regime was first established and the end of the Yuan Dynasty.

From the Kublai reign, agriculture had developed to a great extent. Since Tonghui Canal was excavated from Beijing to Tongzhou, water transportation was developed. Due to paper currency issuance, domestic commerce became prosperous. Cotton planting in south China has become very popular, thus spinning developed accordingly. The handicraft industry and spinning technology developed rapidly. Huang Daopo was among a group of handicraft workers that brought cotton spinning technology to a higher level. Since Yuan Dynasty executed a rather open policy, ocean shipping and foreign trade developed. Quanzhou of Fujian became a major commercial port in the world. This promoted the communication between Europe and China. Economic progress brought along the development of handicraft and commercial trade. The Yuan Dynasty became one of the richest countries in the world.

The white pagoda of Miaoying Temple in Beijing, built by Yuan Emperor Kublai in 1271. It is the most ancient and biggest scale Lama pagoda that still exists in China.

Running Mongolian horse statue in Beijing Yuan Dadu Wall Park. The city wall of the Yuan Capital was built by tamped clay, thus it was also called dust city. Today the city wall still remains in 12 kilometers, outside the city wall is the site of moat. The park is the most important historic site that represents Yuan Capital City's scale, structure, and orientation.

Science and technology, literature and art also underwent great progress during the Yuan Dynasty. Astronomy of the Yuan Dynasty was advanced in the world. Great astronomers existed such as Jamal al Din and Guo Shoujing. Jamal al Din made a globe which assmed the earth to be a round ball. Shoushi Calendar compiled by Guo Shoujing was the most advanced calendar in the world. The Agriculture Book compiled by Wang Zhen was an encyclopedia on agriculture that surpassed all the past works. Medicine was also at a very high level. *The Muslin Prescription* was a collection of all the accomplishments in Chinese history as well as medicines of different ethnic groups. Achievements in literature and arts cannot be ignored either. Guan Hanqing, Wang Shifu, Ma Zhiyuan and Ji Junxiang were representatives in Yuan drama which became a major literary form since Tang and Song poetry. Calligraphers and artists were outstanding as well, represented by Zhao Mengfu.

The Thirteen Ming Tombs and the Governance during the Ming Dynasty

The "thirteen tombs" as they are known popularly in Chinese are the imperial tombs of 13 of the 16 Ming-dynasty (1368–1644) Emperors. The word ling indicates the small mound over a tomb. These tombs or mounds with their graves underneath are located near Tianshou Mountain in Changping County, around 50 kilometers to the northwest of Beijing. The 14 Emperors from Chengzu to Sizong are all buried here, with the

Changling viewed from above.

The Spirit Way of Changling.

exception of Daizong Zhu Qiyu whose Jingtai *Ling* is in the western precincts of Beijing. The other thirteen are here and each has its own name. In chronological order, they are: Changling of Chengzu, Xianling of Renzong, Jingling of Xuanzong, Yuling of Yingzong, Maoling of Xianzong, Tailing of Xiaozong, Kangling of Wuzong, Yongling of Shizong, Zhaoling of Muzong, Dingling of Shenzong, Qingling of Guangzong, Deling of Xizong, and Siling of Sizong.

The tomb district of these thirteen Ming Tombs covers an area of forty square kilometers. The first evidence that one is entering the district is passage through the middle of parallel lines of stone stelae. This is the earliest and best preserved of stelae passageways or "alleys" in China. After the steles is a large gate, which is the proper entryway to the Tomb district. Before the gate is a stele that reads "officials must dismount here." Further on is what is known as the Spirit Way. This is a passageway, 750 meters long, lined on either side with pairs of stone-carved statues of men and animals. There are 18 pairs or 36 sculptures in all. The tradition of placing stone men

and stone animals as an entryway to a tomb dates from 2,000 years ago, from the Qin and Han periods. This was primarily as a form of ornamentation for the grave but also to symbolize the status and protection of a person before his death.

Ling'en Hall of Changling.

At present, one can visit only two of the tombs in the thirteen Ming tombs, which are Changling and Dingling. Changling is the tomb of Chengzu Zhu Di (reigned 1403 –1424, reign name Yongle), and his empresses. It covers ten square meters. The main building above ground at Changling is the Hall of Eminent Favor. This is one of four similar great halls in China, which include the Taihe Hall in the Forbidden City in Beijing, the Dacheng Hall at the Confucian Temple in Shandong at Qufu, and the Hall at the temple at the foot of the mountain at Taishan. At the thirteen tombs, this Ling'en Hall occupies 1,956.44

square meters, which is larger than the Hall in the Forbidden City. Each of the sixty pillars of this massive structure is composed of one single tree. In the Taihe Hall there are a total of 72 pillars, however they are nothing like as precious since they are made of pine whereas those of Ling'en are made of a very valuable wood called "golden nanmu." These pillars have stood untreated by any protective coating for 600 years, and yet they are completely undamaged.

Dingling is situated at the foot of the Dayu mountains, and holds the grave of the Ming Shenzong Emperor (reigned 1572–1620, reign name Wanli), and also his two empresses. The construction of Dingling began in the 12th year of Wanli and continued until the 28th year (1584–1590). The construction expended more than eight million taels of silver, roughly equivalent to two years of national income during the Wanli period, or enough grain for ten

Stone statue of a general at the side of the Spirit Way of Changling.

Five worshipping vessels, including a censer, a pair of candleholders, and a pair of vases, set up especially for the dead. Illustrated is the stone five worshipping vessels in front of the Tailing of Emperor Kangxi of Qing.

million people for one year. The underground palace of Dingling was excavated in 1956. In 1959, the Dingling Museum was officially established.

The Dingling underground palace is at a depth of 27 meters and is composed of five separate halls. It covers 1,195 square meters in area. Three white marble platforms stand in the middle hall. A large glazed ceramic vessel containing oil stands before each, with its accessories of bronze ladle and lamp. A bronze tube once connected the oil to the lamp, but the oil has long since been used up. The rear hall is the largest in the underground palace, being 9.5 meters tall, 30.1 meters long and 9.1 meters wide. Its floor is of polished stone. In the center of the outer wooden coffin is the inner coffin of Zhu Yijun. Xiaoduan and Xiaoqing, the two empresses, are placed to either side, one on the left and one on the right. Arrayed around the three coffins are red lacquer chests full of decorative objects to accompany the afterlife. Some 3,000 objects were recovered from the tomb at the time of excavation, among them a golden crown and a phoenix

Ming-tower of the Yongling.

crown that are priceless treasures.

The thirteen tombs are an outstanding example of China's ancient burial traditions. In China, people have always believed strongly in the peaceful burial of a person after death and funerary customs were an important part of ancient Chinese culture. Generally speaking, an emperor received a first-class tomb, ministers, premiers, and high officials were entitled to a second-class, while officials and large merchants got a third-class tomb. Each had its own standards and specifications, while the common man was glad simply to be placed peacefully in the ground. The tomb of emperors had a Spirit Way placed before the building constructed over the tomb, and on either side of this Spirit Way were Spirit animals and loyal ministers. The main function of the building constructed over the tomb was to serve as a commemorative hall, in which to hold ceremonies and make offerings. On either side were subsidiary halls; there was also a separate pavilion for slaughtering animals. A stele lauding the virtues of the emperor was generally placed. Behind the Hall was a Ming-tower, in the middle of which was a spirit stele. On it was carved the name of the temple of the occupent of the tomb which could be made known only after the emperor had died.

Three of the Ming-dynasty emperors are buried elsewhere. The founding emperor of the dynasty, Ming Taizu, or Zhu Yuanzhang (reigned 1368–1398, reign name Hongwu) is buried in Nanjing at the Xiaoling. Zhu Yuanzhang was a cruel and tyrannical ruler. As soon as he came to power he began to fabricate intrigues and accuse his ministers of plotting rebellion before having them killed. He murdered his chief strategist, Liu Ji. The second advisor or strategist was Li Shanchang, who was also the relative of Zhu Yuanzhang's children. When this strategist was at the advanced age of 77, Zhu Yuanzhang had him killed together with seventy members of his family. The famous General Xu Da was one of the very few who had not been accused of plotting to overthrow the throne. Legend has it that he developed a strange illness and had a particular aversion to eating geese. Zhu Yuanzhang sent an official to deliver a bowl of geese to him, and stayed next

Relic of the Dingling: the gold crest of the emperor.

to him as he ate it. Xu Da died that same day. The Prime Minister Hu Weiyong was the most important assistant to Zhu Yuanzhang, yet Zhu Yuanzhang still wove stories of his plot to rebel. Zhu Yuanzhang said that Hu Weiyong planned to link up with the Japanese in plotting his overthrow. Out of his paranoia, Zhu Yuanzhang is said to have massacred several tens of thousands of people.

Rare hall palace of the Dingling.

The cruelty of the third emperor of the Ming Dynasty was no less than that of his father. The third was Zhu Di. He mobilized a war to seize power from his legally appointed predecessor Zhu Yunwen, the Emperor Jianwen. He killed Zhu Yunwen's ministers Qi Tai, Huang Zicheng, and others, and put to death a loyal Confucian official who refused to write the document allowing him to ascend the throne. Then he obliterated the loyal retainer's entire clan. The successive rulers of the Ming Dynasty were characterized by maniacal cruelty. The character and style of the founding emperor of a dynasty is critical to the dynasty's future success. Other than the rapacious Zhu Yuanzhang and Zhu Di, the rest of the Ming Emperors were mediocre and incapable, some cared nothing for state affairs, others pursued Daoist elixirs. Ruling through the use of spies was a Ming-dynasty specialty. The behavior of such people formed an atmosphere of extreme terror among both officials and common people. Although the reforms of the Prime Minister of Shenzong let in a few rays of hope, they turned out to be like fleeting mist before the eyes. They did little to obstruct the traditional posture of 16 Ming Emperors. Eventually it was up to Li Zicheng and Zhang Xianzhong to start the rebellion that enabled the Manchus to break through the passes from the north and put an end to the Ming Dynasty.

Zheng He's Voyages on the Western Seas: the Glory of a Great Sea Empire

To China, the "western seas" were what is now called the Indian Ocean. Zheng He is the given name of the great Moslem eunuch admiral who led seven fleets out on extensive ocean-going voyages. He lived from 1371 to 1433, his original name was Ma, meaning horse, his "small name" was Sanbao, meaning "three treasures." He was originally from Kunming, Yunnan. In 1382, with his homeland in chaotic upheaval, he was forcefully conscripted into the Ming army and castrated. He later entered the court of the Prince of Yan,

Zheng He's homeland: Sanbao building of Jinning, Yunnan.

No. 6 pond of the dockyard in Nanjing, with relics of grand scale and orderly placed shipbuilding.

before becoming an imperial bodyguard for the Ming Emperor Chengzu, Zhu Di. At the time, countries on both sides of the Indian Ocean were devout believers in Islam, while many South Asian countries were Buddhist. Since Zheng He was an adherent of the Islamic religion, and knew ocean navigation, and since he had been a senior minister inside the court, the Ming Emperor Chengzu selected him to represent him as an official envoy.

For the 28 years from 1405 to 1433, Zheng He made seven trips to what at the time were called the Western Seas. He initiated and cultivated relations and maritime communications between China and 30 countries in Asia and Africa. His fleet crisscrossed the Indian Ocean countless times. He visited India, Persia, and the sacred city of Mecca in Arabia; in Africa he visited Mozambique on the eastern coast. These bold explorations preceded the ocean voyages of other maritime nations by some one hundred years. At its greatest, Zheng He's fleet totaled more than 200 ships. His so-called Treasure Ships could carry goods of more than 1,000 tons. The number of people in just one of his fleets exceeded 27,000 people. He navigated along more than forty primary lines of voyage, and is estimated to have covered 160,000 nautical miles.

The main purposes of Zheng He's voyages were

to suppress the pirate activity in the eastern Ocean, to protect the peaceful environment on the perimeter of the Ming Dynasty and safety on the seas; to develop foreign trade, to promote Chinese civilization, and to cow into submission the so-called Wokou, or Japanese pirates who operated from the 14th to the 16th century in Chinese coastal waters. Representing the Ming Emperor, Zheng He promulgated a humanist tradition of cooperation with allies, and he developed official trade. The famous British historian of science, Joseph Needham, noted that Zheng He's fleet was the most powerful of any at the time and yet did not invade and occupy one inch of another county's territory, nor set up any kind of military povocation to contest borders. It did not plunder the wealth of other countries and in its intercourse with others it adopted a policy of generosity and friendship, so that other countries were glad to submit.

Archaize ship of Zheng He's expedition.

In the third year of Yongle (1405), on the 15th of

Zheng He Memorial Museum and Zheng He's statue in Nanjing.

June, Zheng He began the first of his historic voyages. Travelling with him was a host of personnel including sailors, officials, carpenters, doctors, translators, and so on. The capabilities, preparations, and scale of the fleets were unparalleled in the world at that time. Sixty-two treasure ships held silk, ceramics, gold and silver objects, copper and steel objects, all kinds of products. The ships set sail from Liuhe Town, Taicang, Jiangsu (known as Liujia Port in olden times), they passed through Fujian and Guangdong to the central part of Vietnam, Java, Sri Lanka, Calicut, and other places. The first three voyages primarily visited Southeast Asia: Vietnam, Cambodia, Philippines, Indonesia, Singapore, Malaysia, Thailand, Burma, and Sri Lanka. Each time he arrived in a country, Zheng He would go on shore and pay his visit with the status of an official Chinese envoy. He would extend gifts.

Zheng He's fourth voyage took him to the furthest places, the shores of the Red Sea and the eastern coast of Africa. These voyages were to have a considerable influence on coastal countries that he visited. They stirred up strong interest in visiting Ming-dynasty China and meeting with the emperor. The king and queen of what is now Kalimantan did come to Nanjing to visit, and were received by the Ming Emperor Chengzu, also rulers from Mali in East Africa who personally led a delegation to visit China. Unfortunately, the Mali king died in Fuzhou of illness. In the nineteenth year of the Yongle reign (1421), the envoys of 16 countries arrived in Nanjing. The primary mission of Zheng He's sixth voyage was to return these sixteen emissaries safely to their home countries. On his seventh voyage, he specifically went to visit Mecca, the holy site of the Islam religion. On his return voyage, passing through "Guli" (now India's Calicut), he unfortunately passed away, dying honorably in his post of captain of an ocean-going fleet.

Zheng He's seven voyages strengthened the friendly relations of the Chinese people and the people of Asia and Africa, they displayed the fact that Chinese were building ships and had the various forms of technology necessary for such voyages. They proved that, at that

Zheng He's grave at the southwest side of Niushou Mountain in Nanjing.

time, China occupied the premier position in the world in the field of navigation. Zheng He's voyages were a magnificent feat, representing a high point in efforts at global navigation for that age. The people of many Asian and African countries feel lingering affection for this envoy of Chinese friendship named "sanbao." Today, one can still find traces of his passage: there is a Sanbao City on Java in Indonesia, as well as a Sanbao Mosque, In Thailand there is a Sanbao Temple and a Sanbao Tower.

The emperor who sent Zheng He off on his voyages was intrepid and astute. Zhu Di was the fourth son of Zhu Yuanzhang, the founder of the dynasty. He seized the throne using the pretext of putting down a rebellion. In order to repress any opposition and consolidate his power, his rule was extremely severe. And yet at the same time his reign was characterized by a growing economy and he attempted to establish an open, strong, and unified kingdom. He consolidated his frontiers. After taking power, he made five expeditions into Mongolia, pursuing and attacking the remnants of the Mongol army and relieving the Ming Dynasty of its northern threat. He dredged the Grand Canal, he developed communications, he moved the capital and his military presence to Beijing, becoming the first Han-nationality emperor to establish his capital in that city. Zhu Di focused on restoring a healthy economy and on providing a livelihood for the people. He organized scholars to compile and edit the Yongle Encyclopedia, which contains more than 370 million characters' worth of information. He strengthened and consolidated his methods of rule, he established ruled over national minorities in the northeast. The merits of his reign were many, and it can be said that he presided over a country that was at the time the strongest in the world. The land area of the country under the Ming Dynasty, the area of tillable land, the number of total population, the tonnage carried by fleets, all were number one in the world.

The Shenyang Palace Museum, Witnessing the Transition from Ming to Qing

The Shenyang Palace Museum, as the place is now called, was built by the founder of the Manchu-Qing , Nurhachi, and his son, Huangtaiji (Abahai). It was used as an official palace by Manchu rulers. A previous capital of the Manchus had been in Liaoyang, but in 1625 Nurhachi decided to move to Shenyang and

Chongzheng Hall and the stone kylin at the gate.

building of the new palace was begun. The complex has over one hundred buildings containing more than 500 rooms. It occupies 670,000 square meters in the center of the old part of Shenyang. The buildings inside the palace are well preserved and this constitutes China's second most important grouping of palace halls after the Palace in Beijing. After the Manchu-ruled Qing (1644–1911) moved the capital to Beijing, the palace in Shenyang was renamed and became a subsidiary capital palace. Its architectural style carried on the traditions of ancient Chinese architecture, melding Han, Manchu, and Mongolian arts into one entity. Historically invaluable, in 2005 the Shenyang Palace successfully applied for world cultural heritage site status.

The Chongzheng Hall is the center of the Palace complex. A central axis follows the line from the Daqing Gate to the Qingning Palace, dividing the palace into three parts that run north-south. The central line of the palace contains its primary buildings, with the Chongzheng Hall as its core, where the Emperor managed affairs of state. Various other buildings are secondary to its grandeur. In the rear are the Phoenix Tower and various buildings that housed the royal concubines. The eastern line of buildings has a Great Governing Hall as the main focus, with subsidiary pavilions f o r

Great Governing Hall and the kiosk of ten lords.

Right- and Left-Wing Princes and the Eight Banners. These are also known as the Ten Princely Pavilions. Right and Left in the Manchu heritage referred respectively to West and East, since the worldview of the Manchu faced southward. These buildings symbolized the establishment of rule by the Eight Banners prior to moving "south through the pass" and taking over China. The complex is the only remaining trace of the legacy of the Eight-banner military rule in the architecture of the palace. The Great Governing Hall was used for large ceremonies, such as promulgating imperial edicts, announcing that the army would be moving out on a campaign, receiving the triumphant return of troops and their officers, and enthroning a new emperor. The Ten Princely Pavilions were where the Right and Left-Wing Princes and the Eight Banner heads conducted affairs. This practice of having princes and officials actually work together inside the palace was rare. The Great Hall and the subsidiary Princely Halls form a shape that derives from the Tent Palaces of nomadic tribes. These eleven buildings are in fact the symbolic representation of eleven royal tents: tents are mobile, they can be transferred from one place to another, whereas these Halls and Pavilions are fixed in place. The western line of buildings are anchored by a pavilion called the Wensu Pavilion. Subsidiary buildings include one in which the emperor read the Siku Quanshu (Complete Library in the Four Branches of Literature), an encyclopedic collection of Chinese classical works.

Items exhibited in the Shenyang Palace Museum have primarily been passed down in history from the old Palace, such as the sword of Nurhachi, the "waist-dagger" of Abahai, a deer-horn chair, and so on. In addition, invaluable paintings from masters of both the Ming and Qing dynasties are exhibited here.

The Shenyang Palace is a symbol of the origins of the Manchus, it is witness to the history of the martial tradition of Nurhachi, Abahai, and other Manchu noblemen. It also represents a record of the defeat of the Ming Dynasty in the northwest and the total destruction

The Phoenix building and the roofs around. The Phoenix building used to be the place Huangtaiji held conventions and banquets and it used to be the highest architecture in Shenyang.

of the Ming Dynasty. Nurhachi (1558–1626) played a vital and irreplaceable role in this process of the Manchu rise to power. He was born in Hetu'ala in Xinbin County, Liaoning. His father received a commission from the Ming Dynasty to be Commander of the Left-Protection Capital in Jianzhou. In his youth the father frequented Fushunhu City where he became conversant in both Mongolian and Chinese languages. In 1582, Nurhachi's father died at the hands of a rival Juchen faction. In 1583, the eleventh year of the Wanli reign in the Ming Dynasty, Nurhachi led a revolt that resulted in the gradual unification under his rule of all parts of Jianzhou. He assimilated the western-seas part of the Songhua River region and the eastern-seas parts of the Changbai Mountain region. Controlling all of the northeastern areas, he set up the Eight Banner system. In 1599, he had two of his translators modify the Mongolian script into a more precise transliterating method with the use of diacritical marks, so that it could be used by the Manchu language. In 1616, Nurhachi declared the establishment of a new empire with a reign name of Jin, known to history as Later Jin, in Hetu'ala. The territory of this empire stretched from the eastern ocean to the Liao River, from a river in Mongolia to the north to a river in Korea in the south. "All began a great unification under his rule." In 1618, under the impetus of what were called the Seven Great Grievances, he began a revolt against the Ming Dynasty. He proceeded to defeat

The divine animal at the roof of Qingning Palace.

the Ming armies repeatedly in a number of campaigns. In 1619, the Ming Emperor Chongzhen dispatched an army of 110,000 to attack Nurhachi's capital at Hetu'ala. At the head of the Eight Banners, Nurhachi adopted a military strategy of "You come from all roads, I go from one road," whereby he decisively defeated the Ming army at Sa'erhu. He killed the commander Du Song and annihilated some 60,000 Ming soldiers. In 1625, Nurhachi moved his capital to Shenyang, formerly known as Mukden. In 1626, he personally led a huge force in attacking the Ming further to the south, and was defeated by the Ming general Yuan Chonghuan through the general's use of Portuguese cannon. Nurhachi was wounded and died in battle, although one theory has it that he died from an internal bleeding ulcer. His son, the later Emperor Huangtaiji (1592–1643) officially changed the name of the empire to Qing, but Nurhachi is generally regarded as the founder of the Manchu-ruled Qing empire. Huangtaiji (Abahai) was a genius who combined martial courage and civic intelligence. He was a superb commander and military strategist and in the Sa'erhu campaign he proved his merit. He went on to carry out the work of Nurhachi, consolidating his economic base, drawing in talented people, turning a military victory over the Ming into an irreversible situation leading to the fall of the Ming Dynasty.

Another man is worth mentioning who figured in

the events at the transition between the Ming and Qing dynasties, and that is the general mentioned above, Yuan Chonghuan (1584–1630). His role in fighting the Manchus made him a people's hero in Ming China. He was originally from Teng County in Guangxi, southern China. His ethnic heritage derived from the Dongguan people in Guangdong. He passed the official examinations and was awarded the degree of jinshi in the fourth year of the Wanli reign, the same year in which the Ming armies were defeated at Sa'erhu. Because of this, he determined to join in the glorious defense of the nation. In 1622, he made a reconnaissance on horseback of the military situation north of the pass. On returning to Beijing he asked to be allowed to defend the region east of the Liao River. He rebuilt various cities ithat had been destroyed, including Ningyuan, the modern-day Xingcheng in Liaoning. He made several campaigns against the Latter Jin (Qing) and in 1626 won a great victory in Ningyuan and was promoted to the leading military position of the region. In 1627, Yuan Chonghuan received the rank of Minister of Liaodong, a post bestowed upon him by the Emperor Chongzhen. He was considered supremely capable by the entire military establishment of the country. In 1630, the Manchu Emperor Abahai successfully used the strategem of sowing distrust among his enemies, and the Ming Emperor Chongzhen put Yuan Chonghuan to death by slow dismemberment of his body. The Ming Dynasty thereby lost its great defender, and as a result was totally defeated. The dynasty was

Wood plate that Huangtaiji used to call his armies.

The grave of Yuan Chonghuan, at No.52 on East Huashixie Street of Inner Guangqumen in Beijing.

overturned in 1644 and the Manchu-ruled reign of the Qing Dynasty began.

China is a nation of many different tribes or nationalities of people. In the course of the conflicts and the gradual melding of these people, evaluations of the heroes on either side often result in radically different viewpoints. In the history of the development of the Manchus, both Nurhachi and Abahai were heroes who made tremendous contributions to the advancement and melding of their people. As a protector of the Ming Dynasty, the courageous Yuan Chonghuan was also his nation's hero. In those tumultuous times, each played an outstanding role on the stage of history. Each is worthy of our profound appreciation and remembrance.

The Forbidden City: Symbol of Ancient Chinese Civilization

The Palace Museum in Beijing was previously known as the Purple Forbidden City, when it was the imperial palace of both Ming and Qing dynasties. It is the largest and best preserved group of historic buildings in China. In 1987, it was included in the ranks of UNESCO's World Heritage Sites. The site occupies a total of 720,000 square meters, and includes buildings with some 8,700 rooms. The entire assemblage is surrounded by an imposing protective wall, with watchtowers at the four corners. A moat outside the wall is 52 meters wide and completes the defensive structure of the Palace. The architectural style of the palace itself is majestic and robust, giving an appearance of great strength. It is a masterpiece of ancient Chinese architecture.

The Forbidden City we see today was mainly built

The inside of Wumen Gate and the interior Jinshui River.

in the Qing Dynasty. In 1644, when Emperor Shunzhi arrived in Beijing, most parts of the Forbidden City had been burnt down by the peasant army. After several decades of war, production all over the country underwent heavy wreckage. Thus the emperors of the Qing Dynasty executed many measures to revive the economy. From the middle years of Kangxi (reigned 1662–1722) to the Yongzheng reign (1722–1735) and Qianlong reign (1735–1796), economy fourished and the era was named "flourishing era of Kang and Qian." The flourishing era of Kang and Qian was the last time under control for China's feudal society. The community was stable and rich, with a population over 10 billion for the first time in history. The Qing Dynasty was one of the most powerful empire in the world then. Profit from the flourishing economy, in the thirty-fourth year of Kangxi reign, the reconstruction of the Forbidden City was nearly finished. Emperor Qianlong started large-scale expansion of the Forbidden City during his sixty years reign. From the 18th century till today, the Forbidden City remained what it looked like since then.

Four large gates define the perimeter of the Palace. On the south the official entryway is called the Wu Men, or Meridian Gate. It is colloquially called the Five-Phoenix Tower. Shaped like an upside-down square "U," it includes a primary building in the center large enough to hold nine rooms. Imposing wings flank this central portion with successive tiers of eaves. North of the Wu Men are five arched bridges exquisitely carved from white marble, leading to the Taihe Men. The eastern gate is called Donghua Men; the western gate is called Xihua Men; the northern gate is called Shenwu Men. The palace building arrangement divides the entire complex into

Taihe Hall after snow.

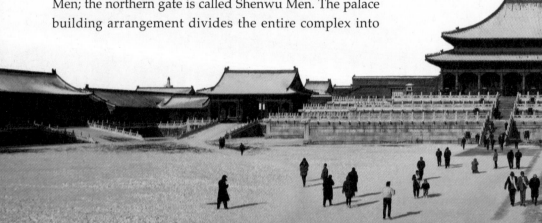

Solarium at the left front side of Taihe Hall, telling time by the shadow from the sun.

external and internal portions.

Three large Halls are the core structures in the "external" portion. They are where the feudal Emperors exercised power, holding lavish ceremonies. The Taihe Hall is built on a white marble platform that stands around five meters high. Carved railings surround it on all four sides, with pilasters that hold carved dragons and phoenixes among clouds. Three tiers of stone steps rise before and behind this platform, with the central tier carved with coiled dragons dancing among billowing waves: this is known as the Imperial Way. In the center of the Hall is the symbol of feudal imperial power, a throne of gilded lacquer with dragons carved into it. The Taihe Hall has ochre-colored walls and golden eaves and is one of the Palace's most magnificent structures. Behind it are the other two main halls of the external part of the Palace, known as the Zhonghe Hall and the Taihe Hall.

The rear part of the Palace is known as the "internal" portion and is where the emperor carried out daily activities and where his concubines lived. The central buildings in this part of the Palace are the Qianqing Palace, the Jiaotai Hall, and the Kunning Palace. Six eastern and six western buildings flank these halls and palaces. The architectural style of the rear part of the Palace is the same as the front part, but the arrangement of buildings is different. The front half presents an appearance that is imposing, majestic, powerful, appropriate to symbolizing an emperor who is highest

The cluster of palaces of the Forbidden City viewed from above.

and almighty. The rear half appears more residential, with each building having a courtyard of its own, with flowers and scholar's studios and places to eat and to rest. Emperor Qianlong lived and conducted his affairs at the very southernmost part of the internal portion of the Palace. Emperor Yongzheng moved his residence to the Yangxin Hall but he continued to conduct affairs here as well, reading memorials, dispatching officials, meeting with ministers. The Jiaotai Hall is located between the Qianqing Palace and the Kunning Palace, signifying the meeting point of heaven and earth and all happy and peaceful things. The Kunning Palace is in the very rear of the "internal portion." This is where the Ming-dynasty empresses lived, although it was made into a site of offerings to the gods during the Qing Dynasty. One room in this Palace is where the Emperor had his bridal suite. To the north of the Kunning Palace is the imperial garden, in which pine and cypress grow and various rare plants are raised. A garden of "grotesque rocks" and pavilions of various styles ornament this rear section of the palace.

There are no trees in the entire southern half of the Palace, since they would block the line of sight and

Zhonghe Hall and Baohe Hall.

"Fair and Square" Plaque in Qianqing Palace
and the emperor's throne.

provide hiding places for anyone scheming to do bad deeds. Only in the most northernmost of the imperial palace can one find trees and flowers.

The outstanding architectural structures of the Palace were accomplished almost exclusively in wood. Yellow-glazed tiles adorn the roofs, white marble is used for platforms. The north-south axis of the central Palace buildings continues a line that extends beyond the Palace area. To the south, the line extends to Yongding Gate; to the North it extends through and is marked by the Drum Tower and the Bell Tower. This conscious placing of the Palace in a central position but also in a continuum is one of the features that scholars of architecture point to as contributing to the harmony, majesty, and grandeur of the overall form of the Palace. The Palace is an expression of the concept of the union of "heavenly will" and the Chinese people. It represents the ancient cultural traditions of the Chinese nation, and is an outstanding accomplishment of craftsmen who were working more than five hundred years ago. The Palace is a symbol and also a distillation of Chinese history and culture. It is a place that any visitor to China must plan to see.

In strolling through the Palace, the first thing to enjoy is the architecture. Secondly, one should view the treasures displayed in the exhibition

Copper censer.

Turret of the Forbidden City

rooms to east and west. The Palace Museum holds more than one million rare and precious objects, or around one-sixth of the total number of documented cultural artifacts in China. Among these are many unique national treasures. Various parts of the Palace display clocks and watches, gems and treasures, and paintings, ceramics, bronzes, and other kinds of art through all dynasties in Chinese history. Gazing at these incomparable works, many visitors are loath to leave. It is advisable for the visitor to allow enough time to enjoy the several thousand years of human creativity exhibited in this Museum. After Qing Dynasty ended, the Forbidden City was turned into a museum in October 1925.

Qianqiu Kiosk of the imperial garden

The Cession and Return of Hong Kong

Hong Kong was ceded to the Great Britain in 1842 and returned to China in 1997. China has undergone its downfall and revival during Hong Kong's colonization of 145 years.

Hong Kong is a unique administrative district in southern China. It is located at the shore of South China Sea, east to the estuary of the Pearl River and south of Shenzhen. Hong Kong is consisted of three parts: Hong Kong Island, Kowloon, and New Territory. The area of Hong Kong is 1,095 square kilometers and its population is 6,900,000. The Great Britain initiated the Opium War with China in 1840 and coerced China to sign the Nanjing Treaty in 1842 which agreed to cede Hong Kong

Hong Kong Convention and Exhibition Center where the ceremony of the handing over of power took place, July 1, 1997.

Looking over Hong
Kong and Kowloon from
Mount Taiping.

Island to the Great Britain permanently. In 1860, the Great
Britain forced China to sign the Beijing Treaty and cede
the south part of Kowloon peninsula permanently. In
1898, the Great Britain forced the China to sign the Treaty
to Expand the Hong Kong Borderline and seized the hold
of the northern part of the Kowloon peninsula which
was named New Territory. The lease was 99 years until
June 30, 1997. The Chinese people have fought against
the above three unequal treaties constantly. During
1982 to 1984, the Chinese government and the British
government have held a series of negotiations and signed
the Announcement on Hong Kong by China and the UK.
The announcement declared that the Chinese government
will resume its dominion on Hong Kong in 1997. On July
1, 1997, the Great Britain returned Hong Kong to China.
The Chinese government carried out policies like "two
systems under one nation" and "Hong Kong governed by
Hong Kong people." The Law on Hong Kong as a Special
Administrative District was enacted. Beside diplomatic
and national defence matters, Hong Kong is administered
by the Hong Kong government. The regime, life mode,
and laws of Hong Kong remain steady.

Hong Kong is a free harbor and has become one of the

most important center of world trade, finance, shipping, tourism, and information both in the Pacific and in the world. The export and machining system of textile, rag trade, electronics, horologe, and plastic have become the mainstream. There are famous universities like Hong Kong University, Hong Kong Chinese University, Hong Kong Science and Techology University. Tourist sites in Hong Kong include commercial districts like Causeway Bay, Sheung Wan, Central, Mong Kok, Tsim Sha Tsui and famous theme parks like the Ocean Park, Big Budha,

Hong Kong Convention and Exhibition Center

Sung Dynasty Village, etc. Hong Kong is worthy of the name Oriental Pearl. Its GDP is the second in Asia, ranking after Japan. It is a competitive and free society in Asia and in the world. Ten years after its return to China, Hong Kong is increasingly closer to the mainland economically and is getting to be even more prosperous. It overcame the Asian finance crisis. The social life has been stable. Its status in the world has got strengthened.

The Opium War pushed China into a colonized state and China started its downfall from then on. With its powerful ships and guns, the Great Britain destroyed the fragile southeast inshore line of defence of the Qing Empire and had defeated the Qing troops all the way to Nanjing. Emperor Daoguang was compelled to sign the Nanjing Treaty. Other world powers followed and threatened China to sign more unequal treaties, cede more land, pay more indemnity, etc. China fell into a period of colonization. The British occupation of Hong Kong for over 100 years was the period of dark ages in Chinese history and also the time of resistance and salvation by the Chinese people. As the imperialist invasion aggravated, continuous disastrous events happened: the allied troop of Britain and France's invasion, the war between China and France, the allied troop of eight powers' invasion, Jiawu War between China and Japan, the 5-30 Massacre, the 9-18 Incident, the 7-7 Incident, etc. Meanwhile, the Chinese people had been aiming to fight for an independent and united nation under the leadership of elites. Significant movements include Lin Zexu's Humen Opium Incident, Westernization Movement, Wuxu Political Reform, Xinhai Revolution, the Great Revolution, the War against Japanese Invasion, the Liberation War, and the founding of the People's Republic of China. The Chinese people eventually achieved the nation's independence.

The triumph in the War against Japanese Invasion, the founding of the People's Republic of China, and the Open and Reform Policy advocated by Deng Xiaoping are three key events in the 20th century that indicate the renaissance of China. As part of the aiti-fascism war all over the world, China's resistance of Japanese invasion started before the European wars from July 7th of 1937 to September 3rd of 1945. During the eight years of war, more than 35 millions of Chinese soldiers and people

The surrender ceremony of the Japanese army was taken place at the Nanjing Army Headquarter Hall and the commander-in-chief of the Japanese army, Okamula Yasuji, sign the capitulation at 9 am on September 9, 1945.

were killed and the loss is over 1,000 billion dollars. The triumph of the War against Japan was the first victory in anti-agression battles in modern Chinese history. Taiwan, which had been colonized by Japan for half a century, was reoccupied eventually. China reappeared on the world stage as a triumphant nation that contributed significantly and gained a prestigious status as the permanent menber of the UN Security Council. The Chinese government wanted to take this opportunity to reoccupy Hong Kong but failed due to limited national power. Hong Kong was taken over by the Great Britain after three years' occupancy by Japan.

In 1946, civil war broke out known as the Liberation War in China. Led by the Communist Party, the People's Liberation Army conquered the Kuomintang army. The Kuomintang government collapsed and Kiang Kai-shek's group fell back to Taiwan. On October 1, 1949, Mao Zedong announced the founding of the People's Republic of China on Tian'anmen Gate. China thus completely broke away from the nightmare of imperialism and achieved independence and liberation. After a century of invasion and wars, the new China is realizing revival of the national economy.

The Cultural Revolution began in 1966 generated a decade of turmoil. The Chinese economy, politics, and culture underwent tremendous perturbation, destruction, and damage. From the year 1978, Deng Xiaoping led this ancient and young nation onto a new era of open and reform and achieved great success. He was also named "the chief designer of the open and reform policy." Deng proposed the idea of "one nation, two system" to solve the problems of Hong Kong, Macao, and Taiwan. This is an innovative way to peaceful realize the unification of China. Deng led the negotiation of the British return of Hong Kong. The two parties agreed on the returning of Hong Kong Island, Kaoloon, and New Territory on July 1, 1997. After the returning of Hong Kong, Macao, which was colonized by Portugal for over 400 years, was also returned to China on December 20, 1999, and became a

special administrative region.

During this period, the productivity of China has developed rapidly. The people's living standard has improved to a great extent. China has undergone deep changes. At present, the GDP of China had advanced to number four, the foreign trade quantity has advanced to number three, and the foreign exchange quantity has become number one in the world. China had achieved spaceflight, constructed grand projects such as the Qinghai-Tibet Railroad, the transportation of gas in the West to the East, Three Gorges Dam, etc. The successful application of the Olympic Games in 2008 inspired great enthusiasm of the Chinese people and enhanced China's influence in the world.

On July 1, 2007, Hong Kong celebrated its tenth anniversary of its return. The policy of "one nation, two systems" proved to be successful.

On July 1, 2007, Hong Kong celebrated its tenth anniversary of its return. More than 5,000 people joined the performance and the audience exceeds tens of thousands of people.

Epilogue:
The Great Wall,
a Symbol of China

Just before we come to the end of the historic journey, allow me to look back at the Chinese civilization in virtue of the Great Wall. The Great Wall went through more than 2,500 years of the Chinese history and bestrides the vast terrain over a dozen of provinces in northern China. It has become a symbol of China.

The Great Wall is a great military fortification project in China that is regarded as a miracle in the history of ancient architecture.

The relic of Han Great Wall in Dunhuang, Gansu.

The Great Wall was first built from the Spring and Autumn and the Warring States periods back in the 5th century BC. The northern states built walls as fortification against each other. In the 3rd century BC, the Qin Emperor unified China and sent Meng Tian with 300,000 troops to drive out the Huns to the north. Meng Tian connected the broken segments of the Great Wall from Liaodong to Linyao of Gansu and continued the construction to prevent aggressions from nomads of the north. Some of it still survived till today. From then on the Qin Emperor has been regarded as the first emperor that built the Great Wall. Throughout the dynasties, the Great Wall has been constructed and reconstructed continually until the middle Ming Dynasty in the 17th century. The whole process lasted two thousand years. The existent Great Wall starts from Jiayu Pass of Gansu and ends at Shanhai Pass of Hebei. The length of the Great Wall is 6,300 kilometers, about 13,000 miles, thus gets its name of "10 thousand miles Great Wall." The construction of the Great Wall is the result of hard labor and sacrifice of

The Great Wall at Jiayu Guan.

The Great Wall at
Mutianyu of Beijing.

Balefire platform.

Chinese people through the dynasties. It had become a symbol of Chinese civilization. In 1987, UNESCO listed the Great Wall as a World Hritage Site. The Great Wall is a must-visit site for tourists worldwide when they come to China and Beijing. Many of them put on T-shirts with Mao Zedong's poetry saying "you are not a man until you climbed up the Great Wall" when they happily ascent the steps of the Great Wall. The experience becomes unforgettable.

View of the city wall of Jiayu Guan from the sky.

The Great Wall is not an isolated rampart. It is an integrated military fortification consisted of passes, enemy watch towers, smoke frusta, etc. The building during the past dynasties all followed the rule of "constructing the forts to be dangerous and difficult according to the terrains." The passes were built either between cloughs and cliffs or at the turn of rivers or at traffic fortresses. In the Ming Dynasty, the fortification system had become extremely rigorous. The wall was built with bricks, with a height of 10 meters and width of 5 meters. There are enemy watch towers every other 30 to 100 meters on the wall. The towers include two kinds, solid and hollow. On solid towers, one can shoot on top only. In hollow towers, soldiers can stay in the underlayers and shoot on top. The watch towers also include rooms for ordinance and forage storage as well as channels for soldier passage. Fortresses in the form of smoke frusta were built on walls on the high mountains. In case war breaks, smoke frustas at the battle front would give alarm and spread rapidly throughout the army. The soldiers run through channels that allow ten persons to pass at the top of the wall, and shoot at the battlement windows. On the traffic main drags along the Great Wall there are passes that were guarded with a large number of forces. For example, in the Ming Dynasty, nine towns